Woman
in the
Water

Memphis Tenn.
June 16, 2006

To Boyd,
This is the story
Of me in Hollywood. Hope
and my family.
You like it.

Dorinda Clifton

Woman
in the
Water

A Memoir of
Growing Up
in
Hollywoodland

by Dorinda Clifton

Permissions acknowledgments appear on pages 273–283.

Portions of this book first appeared, in slightly different form, in the *Bryant Literary Review* and *The Gettysburg Review*.

First edition 2 3 4 5 6 7 8 9

ISBN   0-966501-3-7

Bedbug Press
P.O. Box 39
Brownsville, OR 97327

Cover design and book design by Cheryl McLean
Original drawings by Dorinda Clifton
Text typeset in Goudy Old Style. Titles typeset in Birch.
Printed at United Graphics, Illinois

Contents

Dorinda Clifton

Elmer Clifton

Helen Kiely Clifton

Michael Elmer Clifton

Patricia Kiely Clifton

If two lives join,

there is oft a scar.

Browning

Part 1

Hidden Lives

1

A Confession of Sorts

I'M ADDICTED TO dictionaries. Old dictionaries.

> **addicted,** Given over to, strongly dis-
> posed to, devoted to.

> *A poet's cat, sedate and grave…*
> *Was much **addicted** to inquire*
> *For nooks to which she might retire.*
> Cowper: *The Retired Cat*

My nooks are in hundred-year-old dictionaries. The definitions. The bits and pieces of quotations.

> *We be virgins, and **addicted** to*
> *virginitie.*
> Greene: *Arcadia*

The illustrations talk to me.

> **addicted,** Often used in a bad sense, as addicted to *strong spirits.*

Strong spirits!

> **liqueur,** A *spirituous* liquor made by steeping the essence in the spirit, and afterward distilling.

Spirituous! Spirituous writing! Steeping my words in the spirit! And afterward distilling them onto the page!

This is my ambition.

Gainsborough Hat.

This is my addiction.

Armadillo (*Tolypeutes tricinctus*). *A* Walking; *B* Rolled up.

Of all of my dictionaries, my favorite is *Webster's Thin Paper Edition De Luxe,* 1926. It belonged to my father.

It speaks to me as I always believed he could have, if he would have. Papa's dictionary. It has outlived him by fifty years.

Papa's dictionary. The definitions. The illustrations. They are all part of me as I sit writing this book.

So how to begin?

> **preface,** [prae before fatus—SEE
> FATE.] Something written at the be-
> ginning of a book by way of *explana-*
> *tion.*

By way of explanation? "Explain yourself, Dorinda!" Sister Mother Superior would demand from behind her formidable desk.

> **explain,** [L. explanare to *flatten*; ex out
> & planare to make level.]

I have no explanation. Not for my father's life. Nor my mother's. My sister's. My brother's. Mine. Yet I want to write our story. But how?

> **interpret,** To bring out the meaning of
> something, esp. by *sympathetically*
> *entering into it.*

Can I sympathetically enter into me? Into my father? Into our lives? Where do I start?

I can remember me, a ten-year-old, hiding on the roof of a glassed-in porch on the back of a duplex on Sierra Bonita Avenue in Hollywood, California.

I can enter into me there.

In that place.

At that time.

1938.

2

Girl Hiding

IT'S THE DAY we're moving into the Sierra Bonita house. We change houses about every two years, whenever Mama finds a cheaper place to live. But always in Hollywood.

In the backyard is a big old avocado tree. I'm not supposed to climb avocado trees because the branches might break off. But I stay close to the trunk, and then ease out on a branch, and swing off of it quickly, landing in a private place on the roof that is to be mine as long as we live here. We're just moving in, and already I've found my secret spot! My own place to read, to draw, to be alone.

The porch roof is perfect. The avocado leaves hide me, but I can see people in the backyard just a few feet below me. Also the main roof is higher than the porch roof, the overhang will keep me dry when it rains.

I'm sitting in my place, planning what pillows and things I'll secretly bring up, when I see Papa carrying boxes from the car into the house. Big cardboard boxes that look like they have gone through years of wear and tear. They must have been part of all our other moving days, but I've never seen them before.

Papa doesn't know I'm watching him carrying in all those boxes. Even from up on the roof, I can read Papa's printing on them: NEW ZEALAND. PHILIPPINES. INDIA. CHINA. TIBET.

Papa's trip! Around the world! These boxes could tell me things about the year he sailed around the world!

He never talks about it.

Mama doesn't either.

All I know is what I've heard sprinkled into Mama's long conversations on the telephone.

1924.
Papa hires a sailing ship
With a Captain and Crew.
He takes a Camera Man
And the Camera Man's Wife.
And a Doctor
To take care of Mama
Who is pregnant
With Papa's first-born Daughter
Patricia
Who was born on the ship
Off the coast of New Zealand.

They sail to Faraway Places.
Shooting Papa's film.
Thousands of feet of film.
For the wonderful movies.
That Papa will never make.

How I wished that Papa would tell me about all this. That he would show me what was in the boxes. But he put them away in the back of a deep closet. No light in the closet. I had to use a flashlight to search through them, one by one.

elucidate, To throw light upon.

It will take me to the end of this book to elucidate what those boxes meant to me then. And mean to me now.

At ten years old, I found out what was in the boxes. But not why Papa always hid them out of his sight. Maybe writing the story of our family will throw light on this. And on other things we never talked about in our family.

But what makes me think I can write this book? A book to elucidate us?

It was always *Mama* who did that! Always Mama who threw her light, her luminous searchlight, into the secret, still places in all of us.

Into my father.
Into me.
Into my sister Pat—four years older than I.
Into my brother Michael—four years younger.

It was Mama who explained us to us.

explain, [L. explanare to *flatten*...]

Mænad.—From a Greek polychrome cup preserved at Munich.

mænad, menad (mē′nad), *n.* [⟨ L. *mænas* (*mænad-*), ⟨ Gr. μαινάς (μαιναδ-), raving, frantic; as a noun, a mad woman, mænad; ⟨ μαίνεσθαι, rage, be furious: see *mania*.] **1.** In *Gr. myth.*, a female member of the attendant train of Bacchus; hence, a priestess of Bacchus; one of the women who celebrated the festivals of Bacchus with mad songs and dancing and boisterous courses in gay companies amid the crags of Parnassus and Cithæron, particularly on the occasion of the great triennial Bacchic festival. Hence—**2.** Any woman under the influence of unnatural excitement or frenzy.
mænadic, menadic (mē-nad′ik), *a.* [⟨ *mænad, menad*, + *-ic*.] Pertaining to or like the mænads; furious; raving; bacchantic.

3

A Seventy-two-year-old Inner Tube

THIS MORNING I PHONE my brother, Michael.

He lives in Los Angeles. When I tell him that I'm finally writing my memoir, he says:

"I'll send you the inner tube."

"The inner tube!" Right away I'm back in Hermosa Beach, California! The day my four-year-old brother and I put out to sea. Rub-ba-dub-dub, two kids in a big, black inner tube.

"I still have it!" Michael says. "I'll send it to you!"

I say, "Don't send it."

I don't know if he's kidding or not. It's the kind of thing Michael loves to do. When I was living in Prague, he sent me a package. I opened it up, and there was my blanket! My beautiful, worn, moth-eaten blanket! Pale yellow, with colored lines, here and there, woven into a pattern. I used to think it looked like a Navajo sand painting I saw in a library book about Indians. My old blanket. It's on my bed right now here in Brownsville, Oregon. I can see it while I'm talking on the phone with Michael.

He says, "The inner tube was full of holes. You found an old repair kit to patch it up."

"That repair kit was a disaster! The glue was half-solid. What made me believe in it?"

Michael laughs, "You were trusting in the elements. We could have drowned!"

I say, "Nobody knew what we were doing, two little kids in a garage, patching up that old inner tube, pumping air into it, carrying it off to the ocean!"

"Your aim was to get us far beyond everybody else in the water."

"And you didn't know how to swim yet!"

"And you couldn't kick us back to shore! A man swam out and pulled us in."

"I remember. He was shouting. He wanted to know why Mama wasn't with us on the beach."

Michael says, "He was angry."

"I wouldn't tell him where we lived. I was afraid he'd come tell Mama what I'd done."

Michael says, "We'll talk next time you come to California."

"But, Michael, I'm writing the book now!" (I never can keep my brother talking about our past.) "Tell me what you remember! About the house? Wasn't it three blocks away from the beach? Because rents were cheaper farther away from the ocean? Didn't we walk across the sand and then over railroad tracks?"

Michael says, "The house must have been torn down. When I lived in Hermosa, back in the '70s, I used to drive around looking for it. I never could find it."

I say, "There was ice plant all over the front yard."

"Right! A wood-frame house, shiplap!" (Michael is a designer of custom houses.) "A porch that went all the way across the front. I remember that house."

I say, "Mama was inside. While we two were by ourselves at the beach. What was she doing?"

"Playing housewife. Papa would come on weekends."

"Was she writing?"

"No, she was being mother."

"Being mother?"

Michael laughs. "Playing mother."

mother, n. [ME moder, G. mutter, ICEL. MODHER, SKT. mata, (not found in GOTH where the word for 'mother' was AITHEI and for 'father' ATTA.) 1. A female parent, esp. one of the human race; specif. one's own mother.

For this cause marriage is called matrimony which signifies motherage, because it makes them mothers, which were virgins before.

H. Smith: *Sermons*

2. Source of birth or origin. **3.** *Obs.* **a** The womb. **b** Hysterical passion; hysteria. **4.** Maternal qualities; as tenderness or affection.

5. A vat in which vinegar is made by fermentation.

4

Papa, the Silent Director

Abe Greenberg's Voice of Hollywood

'Down to The Sea in Ships' Showing at 'Silent Movie'

Silent Movie on N. Fairfax is reviving Elmer Clifton's great 1923 epic hit, "Down to the Sea In Ships," which brought film stardom to Clara Bow. It ranks with "The Covered Wagon," "The King of Kings," and "The Birth of a Nation" as one of the super-productions which m a d e movie history and is still the most a u t h e n t i c and spectacular of sea films. It was actually filmed in New Bedford, Mass. (Whaling City, U.S.A.), with real whaling men and nearly all the townspeople participating in typical D. W. Griffith production fashion.

It is unquestionably Elmer Clifton's masterpiece, and is unmatched in its costuming, settings, and photography, and minuteness of details (from the sugar-bowl with the lock on it to the documentary-like authenticity of the thrilling whale hunts, sea storm, and life on shipboard.

The m a n y Griffith-like touches of the film are no accident. Elmer Clifton starred in "The Birth of a Nation" and "Intolerance" and learned directly the arts of the great movie master. Raymond McKee, Marguerite Cortot, and Pat Hartigan are co-starred in this film which skyrocketed Clara Bow to fame.

Elmer Clifton

Aboard ship, shooting Down to the Sea in Ships

DOWN TO THE SEA IN SHIPS was a big success! A hit! Papa made a lot of money!

He and the captain of the whaling ship decided to sail around the world together. Papa would take Alex Penrod, his camera man and good friend! They would make movies in countries where nobody had ever shot film before!

That's what they planned to do. And they did it.

They began the trip in Hawaii.

Elmer Clifton—Royal Hawaiian Hotel, Honolulu, 1924

New Zealand

Nepal

Pakistan

India

Tibet

5

Woman in the Water

NOBODY TALKED ABOUT the world trip. Most of what I know comes from what I found inside the boxes I saw Papa hide away in the back of the deep closet at the Sierra Bonita house. I went into that closet with a flashlight, closed the door, and sorted through the boxes.

Albums and albums of photographs.
Maps.
Scripts.
Costumes.
A white safari hat.

Things Papa would need to make the movies he planned to make out of the film he'd shot all over the world.

The Last Box
I searched through each box. When I got down to the last box, I was disappointed. It seemed crammed full of nothing but old bills, forms, letters about money. Loans Papa had taken out over the years. Loans paid back bit by bit with money squeezed together, borrowed from one loan company to pay back to another, then repeated with another, a never-ending slight of hand.

Seeing the records of this made me wish I was already a star in Hollywood. Look how much money Shirley Temple made! Once I was a star, Papa would never have to be nice to loan company people ever again.

The Last Album

Down at the very bottom of this box was a small tan album that changed my whole idea of who Papa was.

The first thing that surprised me about the album was that there were no pictures of Mama.

There were pictures of a woman with Papa all through the album. But she wasn't Mama.

I remember thinking the woman was very beautiful. But what made me think that? What was I seeing in those old photographs?

I wished the pictures weren't so fuzzy. I wanted to see her face better.

Now, using a magnifying glass, I can see the woman's face is one you'd want to keep looking at—high cheekbones, large eyes, a face with character. Yet not really beautiful.

But maybe the ten-year-old Dorinda saw beauty because she saw love. The pictures still speak to me of the love between my father and this woman.

Even though in most of the pictures, they are not much more than shadows.

I remember how strange it felt to see Papa fooling around, doing fun things, and being with friends!

I'd never seen Papa just having fun.

Papa and the woman seriously playing marbles together!

Hermosa Beach, 1913

The two of them riding the waves! With my magnifying glass I can see a shining, wonderfully happy look on the woman's face.

Hermosa Beach, 1931

I'm a little girl with a bandaged foot, riding on Papa's shoulders. I'm holding onto his forehead with both hands. I'm old enough to walk, but I've hurt my foot.

It's summer. A weekend, because that's when Papa comes from Hollywood to be with us. His coming means at least one walk along the boardwalk to get ice cream cones.

The boardwalk is not like a cement sidewalk, but real wooden boards, about twelve feet long, laid side by side, with an inch in between the boards where the sand drops through.

The sun, high in the sky, makes the big beach umbrellas stand up straight, their shadows, dark circles, right underneath them, in the hot, flat, white sand.

Papa is singing as he walks along. To the rhythm of his long strides.

I am so high up, I feel like I could reach out and touch the globes of the boardwalk lamps. Globes shaped like flames at the top of the cement Greek pillars.

Long before we get to the ice cream stand I can see the giant cutout of the Mile High Ice Cream Cone rising up into the clear sky, almost twice as tall as the flat-roofed building that holds it up. It's bright pink ice cream, not a rounded scoop, but a high, pointed, cornucopia cone, reaching up into the bright blue sky.

I always get pistachio ice cream because of the green color.

We sit together on wood benches watching what kind of ice cream other people choose. I'm always the last to finish my cone. The others are all done, and I'm still licking away.

After ice cream, we walk out on the pier. People hunched over their fishing poles. Fishing lines reaching far below, disappearing into the deep blue.

Smells. Of salt and bait and the blood-stink of fish being washed and cut up in the deep cement sinks, heads and scales in buckets.

Screeching sea gulls. Flying in for landings, squabbling for the leftovers.

Ocean waves. Passing under the pier, frothing up at the pilings, then going on to shore.

Brownsville, Oregon, 2001

And now, here I am, in the little town of Brownsville. Living above the Corner Cafe. One room. One window. Most people in town don't know I'm up here. They don't even know there's space up here to live in. It's like the secret hiding places I used to have as a child.

As I sit at my computer writing this, I can see, out my one second-story window, the roof of a garage across the alley, and above it the tops of trees and also a patch of sky reflected in the mirror by my window.

It's winter now. The sun is playing tricks with the light on the bare branches of the trees. Giving them a magic golden glow. But it doesn't stay. Even as I look, it changes. A cloud I can't see must have moved in front of the sun.

Nothing stays the same.

Hermosa Beach, California, 1913

Papa and the woman in the water. Eighty-eight years ago. Fifteen years before I was born.

There's picture after picture of Papa and the woman in the first half of the small tan album. And then nothing.

Nothing but empty thick black pages. Nothing else in that last box. Nothing in any of the other boxes to give a hint that she even existed.

But I had seen her with Papa in the small album.
And I kept seeing her in my imagination.
But where was she?

Somewhere.
On the beach alone?

I never pictured her with anyone else but Papa.

What was she doing that whole year of 1924?

When Papa was on the ship.
The wind in the sails.
The ship he'd hired.
With the Captain he'd hired.
And the Seamen.
And the Camera Man.
And the Camera Man's Wife.
And the Doctor who came on board
From one of the ports of call
When it was getting near the time
When Mama would have her Baby.

WHEN I WAS TEN, dreaming of the face of the woman in the album, I gave her a name. A name I loved because it belonged to my one friend, Polly Anna.
The friend I lost.

We had known each other in kindergarten and first grade. I never talked about Polly Anna to anyone. Never even spoke her name out loud. That's why I could give her name to the woman in the album.

One of the things I loved about my discovery of the woman I'd named Polly Anna was that she hadn't come to me through Mama. I'd found her. The beautiful woman spoke to me directly from the pages of the photo album. Mama didn't even know that I knew her.

She was my own.

She made me see Papa in a new light. Her light. Not Mama's. And so I named the woman Polly Anna, because I had loved my six-year-old friend, Polly Anna.

Part 2

Was Papa a Happy Man?

6

Head of Orpheus

A Dream in the Night

I'm seeing a face which I cannot see.

I know it is in water at the bottom of a deep well which I am looking down into.

Dream Voice calls out to me:

"Wake up. Open your eyes. And you will see all that is behind the face."

BUT THE DREAM VOICE LIES.

Because when I make myself wake up, when I force open my eyes, the room is pitch black.

I pull the string to the light bulb hanging over my bed.

Light fills my one-room apartment.

But the light doesn't show me the face. The face is gone.

I reach for my pencil and paper. And so I'm writing this at 3:10 in the morning.

I think of the head of Orpheus.

Singing as it swims down the river.

The singing head of Orpheus is in a book I just read by Russell Hoban. I understand the head singing. But swimming? While I was reading the book, the head swimming in the water was no problem for me.

But now, without the magic of Russell Hoban's art spilling over the pages, now it doesn't make sense.

Tomorrow morning, when I read what I'm writing now, what will I make of it?

The face in a deep hole?

Maybe the face is mine.

I've been in a hole for the last week. Instead of writing in my book, I've been writing inquiry letters, submitting bits and pieces of my book to magazines, trying to pass these fragments off as short stories, applying for prizes and grants, pretending I know what my book is all about, as I laboriously fill in the forms of the official application blanks:

> BRIEFLY DESCRIBE THE PROJECT FOR WHICH YOU ARE REQUEST-
> ING FUNDS AND HOW YOUR WRITING ADDRESSES THE GOALS
> OF THE WOMEN WRITERS FELLOWSHIP.

A reasonable request, I mutter to my muse, who hasn't come out of her stupor for a week.

"Wake up," my Dream Voice said.

"Open your eyes and you will see all that is behind the face."

And I obeyed.

And I saw pitch black nothing.

Does a flower bloom in the desert when nobody sees it? Am I really writing a book if nobody ever reads it? Friends don't count as readers. They read you. They don't need you between the covers of a book.

"IF YOU WANT TO BE PUBLISHED," one article in a writer's magazine said, "WRITE SOMETHING GOOD."

It's now 3:30 in the night. Maybe my muse will speak to me in the morning.

Morning Gnomes

There's a door to my one window. Instead of opening it this morning, I stand staring at the designs formed by the natural wood grain and knots, and I see staring back at me the cavernous eyes of two identical gnome faces with elongated pointed foreheads and twin triangle beards stretching down to skinny pinpoints disappearing into the depths of the wood. Tree Spirits caught prisoner when their tree home was felled.

The gnomes look at me. Not speaking.

My muse is still off somewhere. Not speaking.

I decide to phone Michael in California. Maybe something he'll say about the small tan album will get me going.

Michael answers the phone. Maryann, Michael's wife, joins in on another phone. Michael doesn't remember the small tan album.

I say, "Papa seems to be with a theatrical company. He looks so young!"

Michael says, "Mother said he ran away from home at seventeen."

I say, "There's a little picture of his mother on a white horse. Papa never talked about her. Somebody told me she had five husbands. She must have been dead when Papa made his will."

Michael says, "Elmer never made a will."

I say, "He did. I know, because I'm the one who answered the phone when the lawyer called from New York."

"I never knew about a will."

"None of us would have known, if Mama had been home to take the lawyer's phone call."

"Why not?"

"Because the lawyer said the will was made out to Helen Kiely and Patricia Kiely."

"Kiely? Mother's maiden name!" Michael laughs. "Pat was born out of wedlock?"

"And Mama kept it a secret! In one of the photo albums, under a publicity still, Mama's handwriting says: '1922 Helen Kiely (Mrs. Elmer Clifton).'"

"And Pat was born in 1924."

Maryann says, "A hidden life!"

1922 Helen↑ Kiely (Mrs. Elmer Clifton)
Paramount Studios Long Island City N.Y.

Michael says, "Well, we'll never know."

'We'll never know' is what Michael always says when he wants to get off the subject. And I'm always trying to keep him on the subject. I say, "There's a woman with Papa in the small album. I was hoping you would know something about her. This was long before he met Mama."

Michael doesn't answer. I hurry on.

"They must have been very much in love. The energy between the two! I can feel it coming through the old pictures!"

Maryann: "More mystery!"

Michael wants to get off the phone. He doesn't like to talk about the past. He says, "We'll talk when you come next time."

"That won't be until September! I'm writing the book now. Please. Do you know anything about that woman? Papa looks like he was a happy man then."

"Elmer was always a happy man."

"How can you say that? What about all his money troubles?"

"You're right. The bills got him down."

"Mama said he lost a fortune, wasted it, squandered it on the world trip. She said the 1929 crash took the last of it."

"So?" Michael laughs. "If he'd stayed home, he would have lost it all when the banks failed!"

"I never thought of that. But how did he feel all those years making cheap movies?"

"He liked what he did. Remember the Gregory brothers?"

"Two little men in dark suits! Mama said they never paid him enough."

"They probably gave him what they could. Once he made them two Westerns for the price of one! In eight days! He had the camera on the cowboys galloping up the hill. They'd change hats. He'd change the camera angle. And they'd be the villains galloping down the hill. The Gregory brothers loved him!"

Maryann speaks up. "Who was the producer you said wore a cowboy hat?"

"H. A. Lendis!" Michael laughs. "He'd take Papa's movies all over the country. In his Cadillac! Reels of film piled up in the backseat! When one theater was done with the first reel, he'd grab it, race across town to a second theater! Elmer got a kick out of making movies for those characters."

"But Michael," I say. "What about his last movie, *Not Wanted*? That was a terrible time for Papa."

Michael's silence tells me I've said too much.

Maryann says, "Michael, you could write a letter."

I know he won't. I say, "Talking is better! I need to hear your voice."

Maryann says, "Make a tape."

"Make a tape!" I say, knowing I can't keep him on the phone much longer. "Please, make me a tape."

Michael says, "I can do that. I promise. I'll send you a tape."

He promised, so maybe he will.

Papa Was a Happy Man?

What if Michael is right? What if Papa was a happy man all his life.

So where does that leave me? The daughter who was determined to make her father happy? No matter what it cost her?

Papa and Mama, 1930

A Day in the Life of Dorinda

Her steps firm, tears held tight, she gets past the volleyball court, past the kids on the team yelling at her, begging her to stay: "Dorinda! It's the last game of the year! We can't win without you!"

She grips her little suitcase, with its black tights, the ballet shoes patched with tape going around and around to hold them together. The worn toe shoes.

Even Sister Mary Giovanni is pleading with her. "Dorinda, couldn't you miss one dancing lesson?"

All the way to the bus stop, she sees her blurred reflection in the store windows, hurrying along beside her, crying. Nobody understands. Not even Sister Mary Giovanni. Only her dance teachers know that there can be no break in the training.

For eight years.
Monday, Wednesday, Friday, Saturday.
Catch the bus on Hollywood Boulevard.
Take it down Vine. Get off at Melrose.
Walk the two blocks of empty stores. A bar.
A narrow dirty stairway with a sign: HOTEL.
Wait on Larkspur Boulevard.
Transfer onto the streetcar.
Get off at Sixth and Alexandria.

At night, coming home to the Sierra Bonita house, that was the hardest. Coming home in the dark. I'd get off the bus at Highland and Hollywood Boulevard. Walk up one block. Then left five blocks along Franklin to Sierra Bonita.

One night, I told Papa how I hated those five long blocks. Especially where I had to pass MA STAMBURY'S ROOM AND BOARD, the old, falling-down house, with its fir trees in the front yard. And a big solid black bush near the sidewalk. Anybody could have been hiding behind that bush.

Telling all this to Papa felt good, because he was really listening to me. I made it all sound more frightening than it was, because I was hoping he would say he'd come and meet me when I got off the bus at Highland and Hollywood.

But he told me *not* to go up Highland to Franklin, but to walk along Hollywood Boulevard and then up Sierra Bonita.

I remember feeling stupid not to have thought of this for myself. Beyond the Highland bus stop, Hollywood Boulevard turned into a nice neighborhood of rich-looking houses with big sloping lawns and iron fences. No people walking on the sidewalk, but people in cars driving by.

The first time I walked the Hollywood Boulevard way, a shadow rushed up from behind me. I screamed.

But it was my own shadow thrust before me by the headlights of a car coming up behind me. I never got used to those sudden shadows leaping upon me. I'd hold my breath until the car went by and I knew the shadow was my own.

Eight years of classes after school.
And two on Saturday morning.

It was the only way
to win back for Papa
the top Hollywood position
he'd had in the silent days.

I would make him so happy.
He would love me the way he loved Pat.
Mama always said Pat was his favorite.

7

It's Done with Mirrors

IN MY ONE-ROOM APARTMENT are seven mirrors. They play reflections back and forth. They give me the illusion that I'm not looking at solid walls but into all kinds of space within space within space. They multiply my one window.

The big mirror hanging on the right side of my computer gives me a view up the alley to my left that I can't see by just looking straight out my window. The wavy glass mirror shows the top of the telephone pole with its crisscrossing cables sort of quivering like a mirage. Beyond it, a bit of Holloway Hill and the back of an old house, just the attic window and roof rising up out of the trees.

From another angle, my looking glass mirror shows me weeds and stubble and tangled bushes below the old house, slanting down the hill to the side of the garage that has the scars on it.

Enter the Cat!

At first, I think it's a trick of my eyes, an illusion created by the waves in the old glass, but then the shadows, under the bushes, become a cat! It's the large tortoise shell cat, very fat, that is fed by the woman who cooks in the restaurant kitchen below me.

I'm surprised to see the fat cat on the hill. It's usually sleeping in a box outside the back door. It's so big it fills the whole box.

Sometimes there's another cat, a sleek grey cat, that likes to sit on the roof of the garage. I love watching that grey cat silently reigning over all that's happening in the alley.

Now the fat lazy cat is creeping under the bushes. It stops. Freezes. Turns. Goes waddling down the side of the hill. Something frightened it.

When I look in the mirror to see where it's gone, all I see is the white sign facing the one-way traffic on the alley. In the mirror, it reads: ON URHT CIFFART. GNIDAOL DNA GNIDAOLNU ENOZ.

The grey cat reminds me of my cat, Big Grey.

Big Grey

Mama said she was just an alley cat, but I remember thinking she looked like a slim sleek cat I'd seen once in an Egyptian tomb painting.

I loved Big Grey.

We called her Big Grey because when she showed up at our house, we already had a kitten we were calling Little Reddie. Little Reddie was Mama's cat. Mama said she was a Persian.

Big Grey was my cat. No matter what time I got home from dancing class, she'd always come to meet me on the path up to our front door. She'd be there for me, purring, rubbing against my legs. I'd be tired, muscles sore. Again I'd been crying in my ballet class. I never gave up, never left the class, but Miss Frey, my blind-in-one-eye teacher, would say things that made me cry.

But no matter how I felt when I got home, Big Grey was always there to cheer me up. Always seemed to know when I'd be walking up the path.

Then one night she wasn't there. I told myself she was just out hunting. I told myself she'd be there the next night.

But the next night, she wasn't there.

I tried not to, but I started to cry. I went to the study door. It was closed. That meant Papa and Mama were writing. Not to be disturbed. I could hear Mama's typewriter. We kids were never to bother them when the door was closed. But I had to know. I called through the door.

"Mama? Big Grey! She's not here!"

Mama said, "Your dinner's in the oven. We're working."

"But where's Big Grey?"

I heard the typewriter keys start up again.

I DIDN'T BELIEVE Big Grey was gone. I kept expecting her to come home. Every time I saw a cat that looked even a little bit like Big Grey, I'd find myself saying, "Is that you, Big Grey?"

cat, [ME., (F.chat) prob. of Celt origin and akin to L. catulus, Serb. kotiti,] **1.a** It appears to have originated in Egypt probably derived from one of the wild species of north Africa known as the **Caffre cat.** **b.** Of the family Felidae, *the Great Cats,* lion, tiger, cheetah, lynxes, **7.** *His.* In Midieval warfare, a low defensive structure carried on the backs of soldiers when approaching fortifications; also called *cat castle.*

European Lynx (*L. lynx*). (⅓₀)

PART 3

Her Mother's Ring

8

Five O'Clock in the Morning

WINTER.

Night is still happening.

My one window is black. Wet with condensation. Weeping. Usually I can coax open the bottom half, but today it won't budge. Winter makes the wood swell up.

The top half is glued tight by years of paint on paint, including the paint I added four years ago when I moved into this one-room, one-window apartment.

I'm looking at the black, top half of my window, watching cold rivulets dripping, not straight down, but erratic, zigging, zagging aimlessly downward.

A couple of nights ago, I liked the idea of my writing going through a metamorphosis: caterpillar, cocoon, butterfly.

> **butterfly,** An *insect* of the species of lepidoptera, or scaly-winged flies, with four often brightly colored wings, and knobbed feelers.

Now I'm thinking my writing is nothing but an insect! A scaly-winged fly! So what if it's brightly colored? Who cares about its knobbed feelers?

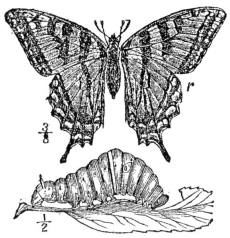

Tiger Swallowtail (*Papilio giaucus*). Imago, with (*r*) Wings reversed to show Markings of underside, and Larva.

butterfly, [A.S. buter-flege, Dut. botervliege.] Why so called is not certain. It may be from appearing at the beginning of the butter season, or because some species are yellow, or because the droppings of some are butter-like. fig.: a gaudily attired trifler, vain, giddy, frivolous.

I'm no writer. I'm a light-headed, giddy trifler.

So? My writing's an insect? Butter-like droppings? A gaudily attired insect? So what! Insects have their place in this world! Even light-headed, giddy insects!

My Destiny

The day I knew I loved writing was the day I made Sister Mary Joseph laugh. My second grade teacher, Sister Mary Joseph. A young woman. With beautiful clear blue eyes. I can still see her. Laughing.

I was standing in front of the five rows of desks, all filled with my classmates looking at me and listening to me recite a poem. I barely got out the last line before I broke up laughing.

I'm a poet.
I don't know it.
My feet show it.
They're long fellows!

Sister Mary Joseph laughed with me. The kids laughed. It was such a good feeling.

MY WRITING IS ME being me. Whatever I be.

And from morning to morning my being is being changed.

A caterpillar creates a cocoon, not knowing what's going to happen inside.

The Philistines inside My Land

All the wells of Abraham…
the Philistines had stopped them, and
filled them with dirt.

Genesis 26:15

Once upon a time, when I was a young girl, on days when the sun was high in the sky, I could look down into my well and see my face in the shining circle of water far below me.

But that was before the Philistines invaded my land. The Philistines who filled up my well with dirt the way they filled Abraham's wells, so he couldn't get to the water.

I remember the day the first Philistine threw the first dirt clod into my well. I must have been about nine years old. I wish I could say it was some-one else, but it was Papa.

I don't know what brought out the Philistine in my Papa that day. I'd made a statue out of thin wire and tinfoil that I'd wound tight around the wire.

I loved my statue. It was a slim, silver dancer. Me. Reaching for the sky. Arms stretched far beyond their limit.

Papa said, "The arms are too long."

Right away I saw my statue through his eyes. The arms *were* too long. I worked and worked to make them right. I kept bending them, twisting them, until finally it was too much for the wires, they broke.

I threw the whole thing away.

I can still remember those slender, silver arms stretching into the sky.

Maybe too many Philistines had been throwing dirt, for too many years, into Papa's well.

I don't know.

I don't know why he went twenty-five years without making another movie like *Down to the Sea in Ships*.

Michael says Papa was a happy man. I say he had to spend too many years making movies for the Philistines.

9

The Voice of the Turtle

THIS MORNING WHEN I first opened the door of my window, a bird began to sing.

The Song of Solomon

> For, lo, the winter is past,
> the rain is over and gone.
> The flowers appear on the earth;
> the time of the singing of birds is come,
> and the voice of the turtle
> is heard in our land.
>
> Song of Solomon 2:11–12

I know most Bible translations say the voice of the turtledove, but I always liked the idea of the Song of Solomon sung in the astonishing, amazing, awe-inspiring voice of a turtle.

Wrestling with My Writing

All the books that teach writing say I must find my **Writer's Voice**. I want to! I'm eager! Each book I pick up, I immediately go for the chapter on The Writer's Voice!

With one voice all the books give dire warnings that until I find my **Writer's Voice**, my writing will never get off the paper and into the heart of the reader.

But how to find **My Voice**?
Where do I look for **My Voice**?
What is this illusive unknown
thing which a writer will be
caught dead without?

Hammer Lock.

What is this thing called love? (Called **Voice**!)
This crazy thing called love? (Called **Voice**!)
Oh, who's to solve this mystery?
Why should it make a fool of me?

Papa's dictionary speaks to me.

> **voice,** n. The *power* to produce
> human utterance or expression.

My voice is my sword.
Shakespeare

Voice gives power! Power to the utterances of the writer who has found it. Here's a definition that came to me in my shower this morning:

MY VOICE
is who I am
on paper.

That sounded great in my shower! But so does my singing voice.

The Voice of the Kookaburra

Maybe it's like a Zen koan? My computer thinks koan is spelled wrong. And I just tried and failed to find koan in my father's dictionary. But I did find what the voice of a KOOKABURRA sounds like! Which may or may not be getting me closer to the truth of what *MY VOICE* should sound like.

> **kookaburra,** n. Native Australian
> bird whose cry resembles hysterical
> laughter.

I can relate to that cry. It's mine when I try to learn how to write by reading books on *HOW TO WRITE*.

The Pitfalls of Point of View

The DO-IT-YOURSELF WRITING BOOKS also warn of another thing I must approach with fear and trembling: POINT OF VIEW. Who's telling the story?

The *First Person I?*

The *Omniscient Point of View?*

The *Third Person He/She/It?*

Or the rarely seen *Second Person You?*

YOU, as in the 1940s scary radio show, *The Inner Sanctum*, with the creepy narrator's spooky voice whispering over the radio waves: "You. You are walking into a dark castle. You hear chains dragging. And suddenly you—"

There's also what's called *Third Person Limited*. I think the *Limited* means that only one person in the story knows what's happening.

After we'd grown up, my sister Pat and my brother Michael often commented that I never knew what was happening in our family.

So, in this story—"Hollywoodland"—the *She* who is *Me* is more limited than most six-year-old little girls.

Maybe writing it from the distance of the *Third Person Limited* might keep the seventy-two-year-old *Me* out of the picture, and bring the story closer to the truth of *Me*, the little girl.

Living on Glen Green Avenue.
In Hollywood, California.

In 1934.

10

Hollywoodland

The Sign

The little girl always wanted to hike up to the sign and touch the letters. From below, they looked to her like huge, fortress walls rising up on the side of the mountain. One day she saw a newspaper picture that showed the letters up close. They were tin! Tin propped up in the back by slanting wooden beams.

The newspaper picture had an arrow pointing to where a young actress had stood on the crossbar of the letter "H" before jumping off. There was an "X" where she'd ended up on a pile of rocks. She'd probably climbed up along the slanting beam at the back, like a monkey scrambling up on two hands and two feet. If she'd wanted to, all she'd had to do was just sit down on the beam and slowly bump herself along backwards down to the ground.

Later the sign lost its last letter. The "D" fell down. So they took down the "LAN" part. And it ended up to be just HOLLYWOOD. Hollywood without the LAND.

The Pond

Pollywogs were up at the top of Glen Green, the one-block-long, dead-end street off Beachwood Canyon Drive where the little girl lived. The polly-wogs were in a big pond with a Weeping Willow tree bending over it, and a life-size, kneeling statue of a lady looking into the water, and bushes growing in and out and around and on top of each other, so it was a secret place where a girl could be hidden. She wasn't supposed to go there.

One day she brought a jar with her. She used a twig to push away the spongy green topping, dipped her jar into the dark water, and came up with five pollywogs wiggling their tails at her.

She took them home, gave them clean water, and hid them under her bed. She knew they would turn into baby frogs overnight.

But in the morning her five little pollywogs were floating on the water without a wiggle. She buried them without telling anybody what she had done.

The Haunted House

Halfway up the street was a little house buried in a tangled jungle of honeysuckle vines. Each blossom had a tiny sip of honey. Most of the time she just smelled the blossoms, because when she picked one to suck out the honey, that was the end of the flower, it would die. Bees could get the honey by just crawling in and out, so the flower could keep on living.

The vines swallowed up most of the haunted house, leaving just a little bit of roof with a stovepipe poking up like a periscope. She wondered if the creeping vines had crawled their way inside through cracks. Would they shrivel up and die inside, in the dark?

She didn't really believe there were ghosts. But she never tried to peek in. If she'd had a friend with her, if Polly Anna could have come to her house, they would have explored it together. But she only saw Polly Anna at school, and there was nobody her age to play with on the block.

Tunnel Vision

She wanted to go to Cherimoya School at the bottom of the canyon where Beachwood Drive met Franklin Avenue, but Mama said she wasn't old enough, so she had to go to another school.

Every morning they'd drive past the kids in the playground behind the crisscross iron fence. She'd try to see everything. But Mama was always going by so fast. Once the maypole flashed before her eyes with a girl on the end of her maypole rope, flying over the heads of all the other kids.

"Mama! Can't we stop? Just for one second?"

But Mama was in a hurry to drop her off at her own school. It was in a house on Franklin Avenue up the steep side of a hill.

Her first day she hadn't known what she was getting into. Mama had parked the car. They'd gotten out at the bottom of cement stairs that went sideways up the hill with a wall holding back the dirt on both sides, too high to see over, like a tunnel with no roof.

When she reached the top of the first flight, the stairs just turned around and kept right on going up between the high walls. She made a joke. "Mama! We're doomed! There's no end!"

At the top of the second flight, the stairs turned around again, and the walls got lower and lower, and then she was at the front porch. She called back, "We're not doomed! We made it!"

But Mama wasn't behind her. She was still down on the street, waving at the teacher in the doorway.

The teacher wasn't waving back.

Mama climbed into the car and went driving around the corner.

Now the teacher was staring like something was very wrong. Right away the little girl knew what it was. The lunch box! It had been her sister's, and was all scratched up. And the picture on it was Cinderella in the magic coach going up the hill to the castle. It wasn't what the little girl would have picked for herself. Every time she looked at the beautiful white horses, she remembered that they would soon turn into mice with pointed teeth, the coach would be a pumpkin that they were pulling around the corner, and Cinderella would be crying, running down the hill with only one shoe.

The teacher in the doorway said, "Don't worry. Your mother will be coming for you at four."

It was never at four. Usually, by the time Mama got there, all the other kids were gone, so the little girl had the swings and the slide to herself. She could even teeter-totter alone by standing in the middle, tipping it one way and then the other.

She was five years old when she started her last year at the tunnel school. She didn't know there were other five-year-old kids already going to kindergarten at the school with the crisscross iron fence. By the time she got there, the ones who should have been her friends in kindergarten were going into first grade. But she didn't know that; she was happy to finally be there.

The Maypole

Her first day she found out the secret of the girl on the maypole. Before you could fly, you had to first walk all the way around the others, lifting your rope over theirs until it was lying on top of all their ropes. Then, when everybody got going, their ropes would make your rope rise up and fly over their heads. You couldn't do it without the other kids.

Inside the playground, watching it up close, it looked very scary. But she knew she wanted to do it. She wanted to be on the end of that rope with the other kids flying her up to the sky.

But she had to wait. Even though she was bigger than most of the kids doing it, the rule was you had to be in second grade to go on the maypole.

She was still in first grade when it was taken down. Only the hole was left. Then the hole got buried during Christmas vacation when the playground was covered over with asphalt.

The kids came back from vacation to find their playground all black.

Everybody said it was good because now the hopscotch squares were painted on the asphalt. She was the only one who sort of missed the feeling of making your own hopscotch squares, bending over, dragging along a sharp rock, digging lines into the dirt.

The three squares.
The two squares side by side.
Then one.
Then the final two.
And then!
Straightening up and seeing…
You'd done the whole thing right.

The Monkey Bars

They took down the maypole because a third grader had let go and landed on her head. It happened during an afternoon recess, so the first graders had already gone home.

She wondered if the monkey bars would be the next to go. Not that she really liked the monkey bars, but they were one of the things she had to make herself do.

She'd climb up and stand on the crossbar, gripping the side poles, getting up her nerve.

Once she stood on that crossbar too long. She had reached up with one hand, got her fingers around the first bar, and then her eyes had locked into that monkey ladder stretching out before her. At that moment, she knew she didn't want to take the first swing out into that long, reaching, grab-bing, bar-by-bar journey through space.

She had just decided to back down when a boy came up behind her, shoved her, so she had to go. She got to the middle and then missed, dan-gling with one arm. She was just inches from getting her other hand up onto the next bar, when the boy came swinging, laughing, knocking her off, churn-ing her into the sawdust.

She got up. Careful to keep her back to him. She knew he wanted to see her tears. She wouldn't let him.

He knew she couldn't tell on him. She'd get in trouble, because she was a first grader. The rule said she was too little for the monkey bars. Even though she wasn't.

Polly Anna

Years later, when she is an old woman, she sometimes wonders if Polly Anna was really her friend's name.

But her memory of long ago is better than the recent past. And anyway, it wasn't like a memory from another time, because Polly Anna has never stopped being her friend, even though they were separated halfway through second grade.

She moved to the other side of Hollywood, and went to a new school, St. Ambrose. That's where she found out that she was too big.

It was her First Holy Communion photograph that made her see this. There she was, smiling, thinking she looked so pretty with all the others. They had white veils held to their heads by wreaths of tiny rosebuds made of narrow, folded-over ribbons sewed onto elastic bands. They held their hands in front of them, sort of like praying, holding little bouquets of roses, not made of ribbon, but real baby roses with fairy fern and paper doilies framing them.

She thought she was like everybody else, but when she saw the photograph, she knew she was all wrong. Her head was sticking way up above all the others! And it was too big!

She wouldn't have felt so bad if she'd had Polly Anna to talk to. Maybe she'd have let herself cry. The last time she and Polly Anna were together, they cried. Just at the very end, when they were saying their last good-byes.

And that's when Polly Anna gave her the cardboard box. It was full of things Polly Anna loved.

Mama's Ring

She put Polly Anna's cardboard box under the wooden ice box on the back screen porch. She thought it would be the perfect hiding place, but it wasn't.

The next morning when she slid out the cardboard box, it was soggy wet. The melting ice had dripped down on it. The lid had caved in.

Inside was a pool of pink water. The color had soaked out of the wooden necklace. The painted face of the pretend wristwatch had washed away. The pretty lady, made of paper on a pin, had come unglued and curled herself up into a tight, stuck-together ball.

Everything was spoiled except a ring. A ring with a green stone. Polly Anna had said it was an emerald.

She took all this to show Mama. Her hands were flat underneath the wet cardboard, holding it together, offering it up for her Mama to see. Just holding it, too choked-up to speak.

Mama reached into the ruin and lifted out the ring. "This is mine," she said. "You took it out of my drawer."

She was so surprised. Numb. She didn't say anything. Her eyes just watched her Mama walk away, putting the ring on her finger.

Mind Tricks

Later, she figured it out. There must have been two rings that were just alike.

But how could that be?

Then she began to think: could she have taken the ring out of Mama's drawer without knowing what she was doing?

Or maybe, she knew what she was doing when she took it. And then forgot?

Could this have happened?

Polly Anna could have told her, but they never saw each other again.

Everything that Polly Anna had given her to remember her by was gone. Out of her hands. But the ring? She'd see it on her Mama's finger. Polly Anna gave her the ring.

Didn't she?

> **metamorphosis,** Change of form,
> shape, substance: esp. by witchcraft or
> magic.

> *The soul…might pass into a deer, a*
> *boar,…a continuous metamorphosical*
> *existence.*
> Martin Wood: *Pagan Ireland*

Last week I came across this photograph from Papa's world trip. Mama with Pat, on a houseboat in India, four years before I was born. Right away, I noticed the ring on Mama's finger.

My first thought was: the green ring!

But even with my magnifying glass I couldn't really get a good look at the ring in the photograph.

> Ring around the rosey,
> a pocket full of posey,
> ashes, ashes,
> all fall down!

There was no reason for me to think of the ring after all these years. But I did.

The saga goes on, circles within circles, Mama loves me, she loves me not.

The Angel that presided o'er my birth
Said, 'Little creature, formed of Joy
  and Mirth,
Go, love without the help of any
  Thing on Earth.'
          Blake: *Ideas of Good and Evil*

11

Outside My Window

SITTING AT MY COMPUTER I can see the grey roof of the one-story house and garage across the alley.

At one corner of the roof is green moss like a small throw rug. In the middle is a metal chimney pipe for a heater. On cold days, when the pipe is letting out steam, the sleek grey cat I love sometimes tiptoes across the roof and sits by the warm metal, calmly surveying her alley kingdom beneath her.

From time to time my second-story window shows me cats, birds, spiders, butterflies, and other creatures of the air, but no people, unless I press my forehead to the glass, and look down.

I'm glad it's this way; I have enough people clamoring around inside me, all speaking at the same time, wanting to be in this book. I imagine four seasons will pass by my window before I and my humming computer get them all down on paper.

This morning my patch of sky showed only grey clouds. I wanted to see if the clouds covered the whole sky, so I stood in front of my window and leaned forward, over my file cabinet, so I could see to the right out my window. The sky was all grey as far as I could see.

The Dead Tree

But what struck me, actually surprised me with a tinge of fear, was the sight of a scraggly, dead tree that I couldn't see without leaning in this awkward position.

The stab of fear was irrational. The dead tree did look like something out of the Hitchcock horror film, *Psycho*. But the fear didn't come from the actual tree I saw. It sprang more from inside me.

This book is taking me into places I didn't know I'd be getting into when I started it. Most of the time I'm very grateful. But this morning, in the grey dawn light, I feel the twisting, scratching skeleton branches of the dead tree reaching out to me. I see my face in the glass of my window staring back at me.

Sometimes the writing makes me feel that all my sensory perceptions are too finely tuned. The tips of my fingers when I type feel like I've taken sandpaper to them. Like Jimmy Valentine, in the old movie, when he was getting ready to crack open the bank safe.

The Dwarf Woman

This morning I must write about the Dwarf Woman. She is part of my story. I've never written about her. Never even talked about her. Not even to the psychologist who presided over the long-ago break-up of my first marriage.

I sit down to my computer.
I see my face.
In the monitor glass.
An old woman.

The old woman sits before her computer. Determined to write about the Dwarf Woman.

As she begins writing, she's aware that she's the only one on the second floor of the old building. The only one in the whole building. The only sound is the humming of her computer.

The old woman hears something. Behind her.

If she lets herself, she'll start believing the Dwarf Woman is standing behind her chair.

The old woman knows she's manufacturing this feeling.

But she doesn't look around.

The Doll House

The old woman actually saw the Dwarf Woman only once. She knows she was three years old at the time because she can still remember the two-story, Spanish style, adobe-color stucco house they were living in then, on Genesee Street below DeLongpre Avenue.

She remembers there was a vacant lot next door with a sandbox. Most vacant lots had pepper trees so there was probably a pepper tree with a skeleton of a tree house riding astride its branches.

The narrow front lawn had a short stubby palm tree. Inside the house, the entry hall had terra cotta tiles that went on up the stairs. The little girl's bedroom was upstairs across the hall from her sister Pat, who was four years older. Her parents' bedroom was downstairs. Her younger brother hadn't been born yet.

The old woman remembers. She remembers herself, as a little girl, living inside the house on Genesee Street.

The little girl is afraid of the dark. It's no use asking her mother to leave on the light. So, the moment her mother switches off the light is the same moment the little girl hides under the covers, flat on her stomach, her hands and arms tucked tight under her.

Across from her bed, on a table in the corner is an old cardboard doll house. It has no front wall so she can see the upstairs bedrooms with miniature beds, dressers, round braided rugs. And the downstairs kitchen, dining room, and living room with little lamps, chairs and a couch facing the fireplace.

The red cellophane of the fireplace has no light behind it. The lamps have no way to shine either. So when her mother turns out the bedroom light, the doll house should go dark like everything else in the room.

But it doesn't.

She only saw this once, by accident, just before she ducked under the covers. That one time she saw the doll house glowing in the dark with a ghostly light that was part of all the other lights in the eyes of the things moving in the dark all around her and under her bed.

She never looks at these dark moving things, but she knows they are there.

She can feel them trying to get her to open her eyes and see them. She never does. She believes if she keeps her eyes shut against them, they won't get her.

She sees them in her dreams, but that isn't as bad as seeing them jammed into the air of her room.

Under the Bed

It's the middle of the night. The little girl has to go to the bathroom. She tries to tell herself she can hold it until morning, but she knows she can't.

The light switch by the bedroom door is too far to reach from her bed. The switch inside the bathroom is the closest. She has to make a run for it through the dark.

She jumps as far from the edge of the bed as she can. She always jumps like this, ever since the time her sister Pat hid under the bed and grabbed her ankle, and the little girl let out such a scream that she couldn't believe it was hers! Even when it kept coming out of her! Mama came and gave her sister Pat a beating.

From that time on, the little girl would jump as far as she could when she had to get in or out of bed. And when she was on the bed, she never let a hand or foot dangle over the edge.

Even now, after all these years, the old woman can't get to sleep if there is any part of her over the edge of the bed.

The Dwarf Woman

The little girl leaps out of bed and plunges through the dark bedroom to the black open door of the bathroom. She reaches her hand up, up into the blackness, feeling all over the wall for the switch.

She finds the switch, turns it on, the bathroom fills with bright white light. The toilet is next to the wall. She gets herself up onto the toilet seat.

And then, between the toilet, where she is sitting, and the bright white wall, standing in the light, close enough to touch her, is the Dwarf Woman.

She is standing. The little girl is sitting, so their eyes are level. The little girl feels the deep black eyes of the Dwarf Woman looking into hers as if they would absorb her into their depths.

The Dwarf Woman never makes a sound. Never moves from her position between the toilet and the wall, even as the little girl, keeping her eyes on the Dwarf Woman, gets herself down off the toilet and backs out of the bathroom never taking her eyes away from the deep black eyes.

The little girl believes that as long as she doesn't look away, the Dwarf Woman can't get her.

PART 4

The Hen, the Tiger, and the Owl

12

The Wherewithal of With

A Dream in the Night

A voice in my dream. It's my muse telling me to memorize the sentence that is unfolding with great power in my dream mind.

I know I have to wake up to write it down, or it will be gone in the morning.

SO UP GO MY EYELIDS. I reach up and pull the string hanging over my bed. On goes the light. I reach for my clipboard and pencil waiting for me on the shelf by my computer. (This is a very small apartment.)

I have the vague impression that the dream was me writing, writing fantastic sentences full of energy. Passion. Rhythm. Images. All rolling onto the pages of my book. But all I can really remember is the sentence the voice of my muse is telling me not to forget. The sentence that was ringing in my ears when I made myself wake up.

I write it down. And go back to sleep.

THE NEXT MORNING I read what I've written!

THE HEN LAYS HER EGGS WITH RELISH.

That was it? Passion? Rhythm? Images?
It doesn't quite do what it did in the dream.

...EGGS WITH RELISH?

The only image that comes to mind is eggs with green pickled relish. Hmmmm.

THE HEN LAYS HER EGGS
WITH RELISH.

Sister Mary Acquila would tell me to analyze it by breaking it down grammatically. She taught us fifth graders to diagram sentences.

I used to love to draw the lines and put all the words in the places where they were supposed to be. It was something that I could have control over. Something neat and tidy that made sense.

My favorite times were when Sister Mary Acquila had us diagram our sentences on the blackboard. Blackboards were black then, with wooden ledges at the bottom to hold the pieces of chalk and the erasers.

I can see myself at the blackboard, looking for the longest piece of chalk, holding it in my fist for a minute, playing like I'm thinking, but actually just getting the chalk warm and soft so that it will come out bright white on the blackboard.

First, I draw a straight line. Then a little perpendicular line right in the middle. I put HEN, the subject, on one side, and LAYS, the predicate, on the other. The modifier, THE, slants down from the HEN.

Now! EGGS, the direct object, goes on the other side of a little fence. The possessive pronoun HER under the EGGS.

All I've got left is the relish.

WITH RELISH! Adverbial phrase! Add it to the verb!

I slant down the line for WITH, then straighten it out to hold the RELISH.

Everything in its right place!

THE HEN LAYS HER EGGS
WITH RELISH.

But. The problem is the relish.

In spite of my nice neat diagram, the sentence sounds like my hen is laying eggs with green pickled relish.

What would my dictionaries tell me? I don't dare look. I'd be cruising the columns for hours.

Ah ha! I know what they would say! RELISH can be a verb! So, the sentence could go:

THE HEN RELISHES LAYING
HER EGGS!

I wonder if she does?

Look how long it takes me to get one sentence to come out right! And how many will there be in this book?

My friend Anton sent me this cat postcard last year. Anton was my husband for one year. He has been my very good friend for thirty years.

City Cat. Young Tiger Cat, Los Angeles, 1948.

On the back he wrote:

> *You must carry a chaos inside you*
> *To give birth to a dancing star.*
>
> Nietzsche

To give birth takes nine months. Will I carry this book nine months?

Tyger Tyger

At first, I had the tiger postcard in front of me. But it kept drawing me into itself. I found myself sort of hypnotized by the eyes. So I put the tiger postcard behind me.

Now, I feel those intense eyes on my back. If Big Grey were my muse, she would be this young tiger watching me from the dark with the light making her whiskers stand out like antennae. One paw with claws showing in the light. The other in the dark except for the claws. When you center in on the eyes, they burn into you. Like Blake's poem.

> *Tyger, tyger, burning bright,*
> *In the forests of the night,*
> *What immortal hand or eye,*
> *Could frame thy fearful symmetry?*

Royal Tiger (*Felis tigris*).
From a photograph by Dixon, London.

Yesterday I found an old book in the Brownsville Library. It was small with gold letters on the binding: *Poems—Blake*. I had a book like that in Hollywood. I took it with me on the bus to my ballet lessons.

> *In what distant deeps or skies*
> *Burnt the fire of thine eyes?*
> *On what wings dare he aspire?*
> *What the hand dare seize the fire?*

My Blake book in Hollywood came off the bookshelves on the back wall of the Santa Monica Salvation Army Store. It was small and black.

This Brownsville book is blue. Worn frayed corners. The binding held together with Scotch tape which is old, opaque, like cataracts.

> *And what shoulder and what art*
> *Could twist the sinews of thy heart?*
> *And, when thy heart began to beat,*
> *What dread hand and what dread feet?*

A thin black ribbon marks the page. The black surprises me. I expect it to be red. My ribbon, holding my place when I was a little girl closing my book to get off the bus in Hollywood, my ribbon was red.

> *What the hammer? what the chain?*
> *In what furnace was thy brain?*
> *What the anvil? what dread grasp*
> *Dare its deadly terrors clasp?*

Pasted on the inside cover of the Brownsville book is a label with ornate printing:

> *The Muses' Library*
>
> *Everett Earle Stanard*
> *Collection*
>
> *Brownsville Community Library*

Beneath this, written in what looks like the wiggly, awkward writing of an old man, is a signature:

Earle Stanard

This book in my hands was once in the hands of Earle Stanard. He wrote his name in it.

There's a street in Brownsville called Stanard Avenue. It's only two blocks long. Streets in Brownsville are named after the original pioneer families. Stanard was one of them.

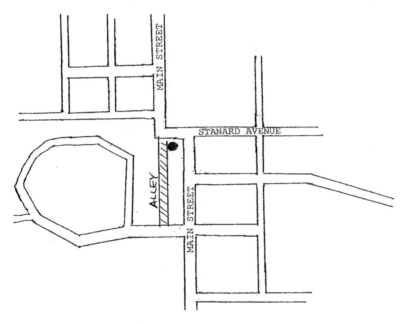

Map of Downtown Brownsville

My one-room, one-window apartment is above the Corner Cafe, on the corner of Main Street and Stanard where Main makes a jog and leaves town.

From 1990 to 1997, I lived in Prague. Then I had to leave Prague and come back to live in Brownsville.

When the stars threw down their spears
And watered heaven with their tears…

Did the "stars throw down their spears" when I had to leave Prague? Did I water heaven with my tears?

Did He smile His work to see?
Did He who made the Lamb make thee?

On the page before the Earle Stanard signature is a long newspaper clipping. The middle is pasted down, and the two ends folded over to fit inside the little book.

WILLIAM BLAKE
By Margaret Scherer

The year 1927 was the hundredth anniversary of the death of William Blake, poet, artist, and mystic, one of the most alluring paradoxes of his own or any age.

This impulsive, unworldly, and independent dreamer could not win wealth or wide popularity. It is even doubtful whether, by any stretch of the imagination, he could have been called a comfortable acquaintance.

Blake and I. And my father? Kindred souls? We three at the bottom of the class when it comes to grasping the fundamentals set forth in the type of books Mama had for sale on the book table at the back of the room where Dr. Litzer lectured every Sunday on Religious Science of Mind at the Hollywood Roosevelt Hotel. *THINK AND GROW RICH! HOW TO WIN FRIENDS AND INFLUENCE PEOPLE!*

Blake walked alone among crowds,
although he held fervently to the
brotherhood of man. And in the city's
roar he dreamed the dreams of lonely
hermits.

For the last four years, ever since I had to come back to Brownsville, I have been like a hermit in my little room above the Corner Cafe. Dreaming myself through this time of metamorphosis. Writing my way through this cocoon period. Waiting for my wings to grow strong enough to fly again.

Blake, glimpsing trees filled with angels
beside London streets.

Seeing through my window the trees rising above the roof of the garage across the alley.

No glimpse so far of angels filling my trees, but for all I know they could be there.

13

A Wise Old Bird

$\frac{1}{12}$

Great Gray
Owl.

YESTERDAY SOMEONE called me wise.

> **wise,** Having the power of discerning
> between what is true and what is false.
> Opposed to *foolish*.

I'm not opposed to being considered foolish. There's a certain freedom
in it.

> *When clouds appear wise men put on*
> *their cloaks.*
>
> Shakespeare

Not me! I've been known to walk half a block in a drizzling rain and not know it.

> **fool,** [ME of *fol.* LAT. *follis.* A pair of bellows, a windbag; pl. *folles,* puffed cheeks; hence transferred to a buffoon.]

> *Experience keeps a dear school,*
> *but fools will learn in no other.*
> > Franklin

> **fool,** One who counterfeits folly, a jester dressed fantastically in motley, with cap and bells and bauble.

I looked up what I'd be if I were "dressed fantastically in motley."

> **motley,** An incongruous mixture of colors. Dress of the professional fool, between 15th and 17th century.

> *Motley's the only wear.*
> > Shakespeare

I looked up *owl* to see what advantages could be found in being the wise old owl. But my dictionaries don't say the owl is any wiser than any of the other birdbrains.

$\frac{1}{16}$

Snowy Owl.

Acadian Owl. (⅐)

$\frac{1}{12}$

European Long-eared Owl.

owl, A nocturnal bird of prey, well known by its doleful hoot, having a large head, small face, raptorial beak, sharp hooked talons. Its outer toe is *reversible*.

A reversible outer toe could have its advantages.

A Motley Mixture of Memorizations

I memorized Blake's "Tyger" on the long bus ride to my ballet lessons. And Hamlet's "To Be or Not To Be." Edgar Allan Poe's "Annabel Lee."

> *The angels, not half so happy in*
> *   heaven,*
> *Went envying her and me —*
> *Yes! — that was the reason (as all men*
> *   know,*
> *In this kingdom by the sea)*
> *That the wind came out of the cloud by*
> *   night,*
> *Chilling and killing my ANNABEL LEE.*

I also memorized the jingles in the advertisements that ran one after the other in a row along the top of the bus windows, each about eighteen inches long, twelve inches high. They changed every thirty days.

HERBATASH HAIR TREATMENT

This had the smiling face of a man with thick curly hair. Next to him a sad-eyed man peering into the mirror at his shiny, round, bald head. The slogan said:

"TOO LATE FOR HERBATASH!"

Now nobody knows what I mean when I say this. But I say it anyway.

SERUTAN

This had a brown bottle with a label that said it contained the power to "KEEP YOU REGULAR."

"SERUTAN IS NATURE'S
SPELLED BACKWARDS"

Why am I putting these gems of advertising in my book? Maybe because they've stayed with me all these years.

When I started writing, I was hoping the book would elucidate my life. My father. My family. I'm not so sure that's what's happening. But I press on. Regardless.

Press on! Regardless! That's a phrase my first husband and I heard when we were on our honeymoon. For three months we rode all over Europe on a motorcycle and sidecar. We wanted to travel like the Europeans did. It was just after World War II. Not many cars.

We ended our trip touring England. By that time we'd just about run out of money. So we sold the sidecar, and I rode on the motorcycle seat holding onto Bill, with two suitcases and a cuckoo clock piled up behind me. It rained a lot.

Once we were winding along a country road, no shelter in sight, and suddenly a downpour. The rain pounded down on us. We kept going. The next town was a long way off.

Then, at a bend in the road, a teashop! We parked in front of it beside another motorcycle.

Inside was cozy and warm. We had tea and crumpets. The only other customer was an Englishman sitting at a little table with his empty tea cup and crumpet crumbs before him. We talked from our table to his.

Outside the rain kept pouring down.

Finally the Englishman stood up, paid, put on his motorcycle gear, and went striding purposefully toward the door. As he went out, he called back over his shoulder to us: "Press on! Regardless!"

We sat watching him through the rain-soaked windowpane.

He ran. Dodging the biggest puddles. Mounted his motorcycle. Brought all his weight down on the starter pedal. Once! Twice! Three times! Four times!

We held our breath!

The motor caught! Roared to life!

Off he went!

We watched him disappear into the solid sheets of water.

Then *we* went dashing, splashing to *our* motorcycle, calling out to each other: "Press on! Regardless!"

Lion.

PART 5

Scars

14

My Brother Michael

I'VE PROMISED MYSELF that every morning, when I open the door to my window, the next thing I'll do is start writing.

This morning I didn't want to start the day. But I dutifully went through my morning rituals and then pushed back the latch and swung open the door to my second-story window.

Winter.

I came close to the window with my coffee. I don't know why I do this now and then. It always seems to show me things I don't want to see. I'm too sensitized by this book.

Today it's the frost. It's sticking to the scars on the side of the garage across the alley. Years ago, a car must have scraped along and dug out the plaster. Deep gashes that nobody has ever done anything about.

Frost makes them look puffed up.

Like the healed scars on my brother's back.

My brother's back has a network of bunched-up skin that looks like he's had a terrible whipping.

> **scar, 1.** To disfigure by inflicting a wound.

I hate to see these reminders of our past. Once I asked him why he didn't have the scars removed. Why should I, he said, they don't bother me.

scar, 2. Any mark resulting from in-
jury, material or moral.

We were living in the El Capitan Apartments in Hollywood. Four stories high with an underground garage. I can almost smell the dark cement of that garage, cool and mysterious, with big pillars that held up the whole building. We kids weren't supposed to play in the garage, but we did. We played wherever we wanted in the big old apartment house.

At the front of the building were tall, skinny palm trees growing up out of a narrow strip of lawn, between the sidewalk and the street. The tops of the palms reached almost to what looked like a tile roof. But it wasn't.

It was a false roof, just three feet of tiles running along the front edge of the building. Hidden behind this fake tile roof was the real roof. It was flat, black asphalt that got sticky hot in summer. You couldn't see it from the street.

That flat roof was one of my secret places. Nobody ever saw me going up there. I'd take the last flight of stairs that ended in a big fire door, very heavy, but it had a sort of plunger that I threw my whole body against to make it open.

I'd sit in a shady spot. I remember one of the books I read up there. It was very big and thick. A fairytale called *Water Babies*.

Sometimes I'd stand up and peek over the edge at the rear of the build-ing. I could see the swimming pool four stories down with all the kids there. I loved being down there with them, but I also loved being in my secret places reading.

When it rained my hiding place was inside the apartment building un-derneath a certain stairway. I liked the feel of the carpet there, it was soft and thick, not worn down the way it was where people walked in the hall-ways. People couldn't see me under the stairs when they walked by.

scar, 3. A mark left on a stem or branch
by the fall of a leaf.

All these years I've wondered how that car could have dragged my little brother. I was at the pool that day. I knew he was running for the ball. But I never knew it would take him all the way down that long narrow passageway along the side of the building.

A few years ago, Michael told me he went back to look at the pool. "I always thought it was so big," he said. "It was only twenty feet wide! And not much longer! The whole thing crammed between the edge of the property and the back of the apartment building."

I asked him how long the passageway to the street was, but he hadn't noticed.

I'll not go back to look. But I know the passageway was very long. I don't know how that bouncing ball went so far. Michael must have kicked it by accident while he was running after it.

He was just an excited little kid, his bare foot could have hit it while he was chasing it. That ball couldn't have kept going all that way on its own.

I remember how I went running down that passageway and came out at the street to see my little brother standing in front of Mr. Manning on the narrow strip of lawn between the apartment house and the street.

Mr. Manning was kneeling, his hands around my brother's waist, holding him up. My little brother was so skinny, Mr. Manning's big hands could have gone all the way around him.

I must have seen my brother's back with the flesh all ripped off. But I don't remember that.

If only Michael had been wearing clothes. But his whole body was bare except for his thin little trunks. We kids were all wearing our bathing suits, standing around on the strip of lawn and the sidewalk. Standing around Mr. Manning who was kneeling in front of my little brother.

I heard people talking. "The woman was looking for an address." "Going slow." "Dragged the poor kid along on his back." "Torn! Down to the bone."

I remember running up the three flights of stairs to get Mama. I could go faster than the elevators. When I ran into the apartment, she said: "It was your job to keep an eye on him."

Mr. Manning

We kids always thought Mr. Manning was rich because whenever he was at the pool, he treated everybody to Good Humor Bars. The pool was too far away from the street to hear the Good Humor bell, so the Good Humor Man would park his truck and come along the passageway to the pool.

Mr. Manning would always buy ice cream for everybody. He'd be sitting in his beach chair with the Good Humor Man standing over him, taking his order, and the orders of the adults around him.

Then Mr. Manning would wave at us kids to go, and we'd follow the Good Humor Man down the passageway and out to the street where we'd crowd around his Good Humor truck with its big shiny sign with colored pictures of all the different kinds of ice cream bars. We kids could pick whatever we wanted. Not just the chocolate-covered vanilla. But sugary pink sprinkled all over with coconut. Or dark chocolate with crumbled nuts sticking to it.

I was so glad Mr. Manning was kneeling talking to my brother. Over the years I've figured out that kneeling, holding up my brother, was all Mr. Manning could do. He couldn't lay the little kid down on his tummy on the lawn. He couldn't even put anything around him to stop the shivering. Nothing could touch that back.

I can still hear Mama's voice: "It was your job to keep an eye on him." Those were her words when I ran into the apartment to get her to come down.

"It was your job to keep an eye on him."

I was shocked. I never knew I was supposed to be watching him. Didn't Mama know that lots of times I wasn't even at the pool? That I was in my secret hiding places? Up on the roof? Under the stairs?

"It was your job to keep an eye on him."

It was my job and I hadn't done it. Every time I saw my brother's scars, I'd remember this.

> **scar, 4**. A lasting effect of an injury sustained, as a dishonor, a lapse of integrity, or a wound to the feelings by affliction, grievous loss, or disappointment, or the like.

15

A Cloister of Sorts

Cloister of Las Huelgas, Burgos, Spain.

MY ONE ROOM.

The entrance is up narrow, turning stairs.

You have to come through the kitchen of the Corner Cafe. A commercial kitchen so it's against health laws for the public to walk through. I'm the only one who comes in and goes out of my hermitage. Thomas Merton would have approved of it. My secret place.

I walk through the busy kitchen
Alone
Climb my narrow, turning stairs
To the loft above.

Narrow, winding, stone stairs
Spiraling around and around
To the choir loft of
Blessed Sacrament Cathedral
On Sunset Boulevard
In Hollywood.

In Brownsville.
Upstairs in my one room.
No TV. No VCR. No phone.
My computer and I do not Internet.
I do not connect to the outside.
Except through my one window.

So I'm very private up here
For the last four years
In my one room cocoon.
The experienced old butterfly
Turning into a neophyte writer.

neophyte, [L. *neophytus,* fr. Gr. newly
planted.] Newly come into being; a
novice.

After Baptism in the ancient church,
the neophyte partook of milk and
honey.
                              Encyc. Brit. III

An Irish Wake

Once I was talking to Michael about Mama. How she left us three kids so much on our own.

I said, "I think Mama raised us the way she was raised. I've been reading about the Irish immigrants. About their lives in the slums of New York. Their kids were out on the streets all day and into the night. Their parents never knew where they were."

"We were pretty much on our own," Michael admitted.

"So was Mama!" I said. "Born of poor Irish Catholics in Brooklyn!"

Michael didn't think this had affected Mama's way of raising us. "Donald White was the same way."

Donald White was the boy who lived kitty-corner from us on Grace Avenue. I was the oldest, Don White two years younger, Michael a year younger than Don. We three were the only kids in our neighborhood. Whenever I wasn't at my dancing lessons, we three were together.

We dug a tunnel into the side of the hill that came out in Don's yard. We went on long hikes into the canyons and hills of Hollywood.

One day we were climbing a cliff in an abandoned stone quarry. I kept going higher and higher, Don and Michael wouldn't follow me. I kept calling them chicken, until I got stuck. I panicked. Was afraid to move. Felt dizzy when I looked down.

I was there, frozen, when an older boy came into the quarry. Michael and Don asked him to help me. By then I couldn't speak.

He climbed up until he was directly beneath me on the steep trail. He talked to me as he took one of my feet in his hand, gently put it in a safe place below, and then the other foot.

When I came to a ledge, he had me take off my shoes; they were making me slip. I threw them down the cliff without looking.

Unfortunately they landed on another high place. When I was safely down, Michael and Don wanted me to just leave the shoes. And so did the older boy. But I knew Mama would be angry if I came home without my shoes. So I climbed up to get them. All three boys came with me.

We talked the boy into coming home with us. I told him my mother would want to thank him.

Mama must have seen us coming because she opened the front door when we were halfway up the path.

I tried to tell her what the boy had done. But she wouldn't let me. For some reason she was angry at him.

I felt terrible. She ordered Michael and me into the house. Don White hurried home.

From my bedroom window I saw the boy walking down Grace Avenue hill.

I still don't know what made Mama so angry at him.

I don't know what was going on with Mama.

I'm beginning to think she didn't either.

Maybe she was like me. So often I don't know what effect I'm having on people. I've learned to ask. But I don't think Mama ever knew there was anything to ask about.

And I do think it all had to do with the way she was raised. But I'll never know. She used to say I was mentally off. And maybe I was. And maybe she was too.

A couple of years ago, Michael drove back to that quarry. He told me that it looked just as high to him as an adult as it had looked to him that day as a boy.

AFTER MAMA DIED, I put off writing the story of our family.

For years.

It was probably mainly because I was having such fun traveling the world.

But then I found myself back in Brownsville. In this one- room, one-window apartment that's like one of my old hiding places.

Not many people know I'm up here writing and laughing and crying myself through the pages of this book—an Irish wake for Papa. And for Mama. And for Pat.

Now it's just Michael and I left.

Dorinda and Michael, Hermosa Beach

16

My Sister Pat

My Hundred-Year-Old Window

The glass came to Brownsville by covered wagon on the Oregon Trail. A section of this wagon trail can still be seen along the foothills of Brownsville. Sometimes when I'm hiking, I follow the route the covered wagons took.

My window glass came in barrels of flour. The stained-glass windows for the San Francisco mission came by ship in barrels of molasses.

> **glass,** n. 1. A hard, brittle, and commonly transparent, amorphous substance made by fusing together some form of silica, as sand.

> **silica,** n. *Chem.* Silicon dioxide, occurring naturally as quartz and opal.

> **opal,** n. *Min.* An amorphous form of silica… The **noble** opal, harlequin opal, **black** opal, **fire** opal.

My hundred-year-old glass is made of sand fused together. Maybe with grains of minuscule noble or fire opal. Glass was made in Egypt over 4,000 years ago. I wonder who first discovered how to make it.

In 1958 I designed a house with large plate glass windows and sliding glass doors. My first husband and I built this house at Corona Del Mar,

California. We lived there with our three boys for fourteen years. It was a good home for all of us. The California windows brought the outdoors, indoors.

My Oregon window doesn't do this. The inside and the outside are two separate worlds. I'm inside looking out. What I see is limited by what comes through the glass.

JUST NOTICED my window is on my ceiling.

Opal reflections.
Moving light.
Fading.
Sun moving.
Evanescent.

I look again.
It's gone.

> evanescence, [fr. vanus empty, insubstantial.] To fade out of sight, melt into thin air, disappear. A state of being lost to view.

> *The great principles of truth…fade*
> *at last in total evanescence.*
> Samuel Johnson

Sleeping on the Roof

I used to try to pinpoint the exact moment when a morning star vanished from the sky.

I'd be lying on the porch roof of our Grace Avenue house on the hill overlooking Hollywood. In the brief time when the night and the day met, I'd keep my eyes glued to one star, determined to identify precisely when it went out, when it disappeared into the day sky.

I'd keep seeing it. Then I'd be seeing blank sky.

The roof was flat, tar paper, over a glassed-in front porch. At one corner the tips of the arching palm fronds touched the flat roof.

Every once in a while one of us kids would decide to sleep out there. We'd climb out onto the roof through the dormer window in the upstairs hall. Our bedrooms were upstairs. Papa and Mama slept downstairs. They didn't know we were sleeping on the roof.

I loved to sleep on the roof. For some reason I wasn't afraid of the dark when I was sleeping outside. I'd drag a pad and my blanket and pillow through the window.

All those nights I slept there, I didn't know that rats used the palm fronds as bridges to get from the palm trees to our house. Maybe I heard them in the palms, but just thought they were night birds.

In the morning, the tar-paper roof all around me would be wet with dew. And so would my bedding. I'd leave it there for the sun to dry it out. As I headed back to the window, my bare feet would make a path of footprints in the dew.

No More Sky Watching

Our sleeping on the roof ended on the night Michael had to tell Mama and Papa that Pat was sleeping out there.

It was a night when Pat came home from a date with Kenny. Michael and I were sleeping in our beds. Pat climbed out on the roof to sleep.

I woke up hearing Mama downstairs screaming on the phone to Kenny's mother. Michael woke up, too. It was three o'clock in the morning. I don't know why Mama had decided to make sure Pat was home and sleeping in her bed.

We heard Papa trying to calm Mama down.

Then we heard Mama screaming at Kenny's father on the phone!

I didn't know what Mama was so angry about.

But Michael knew.

He looked out the window.

Pat was on the flat roof, sleeping through the whole thing.

Michael ran downstairs and told Papa.

After that we kids couldn't sleep on the roof anymore.

> *...as the evanescence of mist or dew;*
> *the evanescence of earthly hopes.*

Years Later

A meeting. Pat and I. About halfway through our lives. Pat is 46. I am 42. We are having coffee in Pat's kitchen.

I say, "I think I remember a walk-in closet. But maybe it was a dream. It's such a fleeting memory."

Pat is upset with me. "It was *real*! I was locked inside that walk-in closet! With Mama! She was using a wire coat-hanger on me! That's when we were living at the El Capitan Apartments."

Pat is staring at me.

"Dorinda! How could you forget? You were eight years old! I was twelve! It was the night before my Confirmation!"

I look away from her. I'm beginning to remember.

"Mama had me locked inside with her! I couldn't get out the door!"

I see myself standing outside that closet door.

Now Pat is shouting at me, "My Confirmation dress was hanging inside the closet! I got blood all over it! Mama was so mad, she made me wear it that way the next day!"

I'm there at that door hearing what's happening inside. Then tiptoeing away. Telling myself that I will always be so good, so very good, that what is happening to Pat inside will never happen to me.

Pat says, "I had to walk down the aisle of the church wearing that dress! You were up in the choir loft!"

The choir loft. High up by the vaulted ceiling of Blessed Sacrament on Sunset Boulevard in Hollywood. Singing in the children's choir.

With Mr. Biggs playing the organ.

Sister Mary Giovanni leading us, waving her arms, her black veil flying around her.

Our voices lifting with hers, soaring far beyond ourselves.

Kyrie eleison. Christe eleison.

Communion was my favorite time. I loved coming down from the choir loft with the other kids, one after the other, down the narrow, winding stairway that went round and round the central pillar, and then all of us in a single line walking slowly down the long center aisle to kneel at the altar for Holy Communion.

I have good memories of Blessed Sacrament.

I have no recollection of Pat's Confirmation.

Inside the Tree House

The day Pat and I were talking in her kitchen, she told me about other times that I should have remembered. She showed me snapshots of the Grace Avenue house.

She said Mama had bought it without telling Papa. She did it during the short time when we had lots of money. Papa had sold the rights to his silent movie *Down to the Sea in Ships* to Twentieth Century Fox. He was hired to be one of the writers on the new script. He thought he'd be working at Fox for a long time.

Mama didn't believe it would last. So when Papa gave her five hundred dollars to buy herself clothes, she secretly bought the old house on the hill overlooking Hollywood Boulevard. It was in such bad shape that $500 was enough for a down payment. We moved there when Papa lost his job at Fox. It was the last house we lived in as a family.

Pat showed me a snapshot she had taken of the tree house we kids had built in the backyard. Her photo made it look like an awkward, abstract sculpture perched in the scrawny branches of the old pepper tree. I can remember the smell of the leaves and peppers, and the lumber we'd sawed, and the tar-paper roof baking in the hot sun.

One day we three were up inside the tree house, huddled together. We'd pulled up the rope and closed the trapdoor. We could hear Mama in the house, screaming, slamming doors.

Pat giggled and said, "Mama's on the warpath, and we're the Indians!"

MOST OF THE TIMES when Mama was in one of her rages, Papa would get into his Lincoln convertible and drive away.

But one day Papa took Pat with him.

She was seventeen years old. I remember how pale and quiet my sister looked sitting in the backseat of Papa's convertible. The top was down.

Mama was up in Pat's bedroom yelling and throwing things out Pat's window.

I remember how shocking it felt to see Pat's clothes come flying out her bedroom window, landing in Papa's garden, getting stuck on the rose bushes.

I was running around, trying to gather them up. I really believed that if I could get all Pat's things back into the house, everything would be all right.

Mama kept throwing things.

Things Pat had been saving in her Hope Chest for her marriage to Kenny.

Embroidered sheets for their bed.
Dishes breaking as they landed.
A box of silverware
flying open in the air
raining down
spoons,
forks,
knives.

I'm crying as I write this now. But I didn't cry then. Even when Papa started backing the car down the driveway, I didn't think he was taking my sister away.

PAPA TOOK PAT to live with Aunt Grace and Uncle Hilton. Uncle Hilton was a cripple. He couldn't walk or bend his back. Aunt Grace had fallen in love with Uncle Hilton when she was his nurse in the hospital after his accident. Papa used to say being a cripple hadn't made Uncle Hilton lose his sense of humor.

I didn't see Pat again for four years. By then she had married Kenny and had Kristine and Kenny Jr. and they were living in their tract house. Kenny worked all his life for the telephone company.

Peace Without Pat

Mama didn't explode anymore, now that Pat wasn't lighting her fuse.

I didn't tell myself I was missing Pat. Maybe I didn't know I was. I do remember what it felt like, to have Sunday family dinner without Pat.

My job was to set the big round oak table. I'd start out by counting five plates. Even after Pat had been gone a long time, I still found myself counting and taking down five dinner plates out of the cupboard.

I'd walk around the table carefully setting them out in their proper places. Then I'd stop still, wondering what was wrong.

I might stand there a whole minute. Then it would come to me. Only four of us now. I'd feel stupid. Wouldn't say anything to anyone. I'd put the plate back, and change things around so Pat's empty place wouldn't show.

Sunday dinners, when Pat was with us, we'd always hold hands and sing our song, pumping our hands up and down, five of us, we kids singing as loud as we could.

Oh, the Cliftons, the Cliftons.
We have a lot of fun.
We let it rain or shine.
Oh, the Cliftons,
A merry, merry, merry lot are we!
Diddle-ee-um. Bum bum.

Then we'd kiss the hand on our right and then the hand on our left. We didn't do that after Pat was gone.

17

Water No Longer Magic

A Dream in the Night

I am thrilled that my sister Pat is wildly riding bareback on a white horse across the rippling water of the ocean.

I am happily racing on foot ahead of the galloping white horse.

But suddenly I see that the water is no longer water. The ripple waves have turned into white plaster of Paris stretching to the far horizon. Plaster of Paris, the material that cheap statues are made of.

I try to warn my sister: "Slow down, slow down." Now that the white horse is not galloping on water, it is no longer safe.

I make my words like a chant, hoping the slow rhythm will reach her:

"Slow down. Slow down. Slow down."

But the white horse, running without her, comes racing by me. Eyes rolling, mouth frothing.

I see its beautiful, smooth, white back as it gallops away.

I see my sister thrown down on her stomach on the rippling plaster of Paris.

I WAKE UP THINKING that everything in my dream is me.

I am my sister.

I am the water, alive, sparkling.

I am the white horse whose galloping is my writing.

I am the water turned to cheap plaster of Paris.

I am the runner, racing on foot ahead of the horse.

I am the prophet Elijah, running ahead of Ahab's horses. The prophet who knows that the riding is no longer happening on magical water.

Out My Window

I see a dangling telephone cable, thick, black, waving up and down in the wind! It scares me. It's always been still and straight and stretched across the sky at the upper edge of my window.

Then, along the bottom edge of my second-story window, I see the white top of the cab of a truck as it drives by, and then the crooked elbow of a crane holding a man standing in the bucket. Hard hat. Bright orange vest.

He goes by in the air without looking my way.

His eyes are on the dangling cable.

WHEN KENNY MARRIED Pat, his job at the telephone company was climbing up the utility poles and hanging by a strap around his waist, as he took care of the wires.

After a few years, he was promoted to work inside behind a counter, handing out supplies to the ones who worked up in the air.

Pat was happy when her husband's job was safe inside. I wonder if he ever missed working outside, up in the air.

Kenny died while I was living in Prague. I had a job there, working with young theater people. We toured with our plays all over Europe.

I didn't know about Kenny's death until the next time I had a stopover in Los Angeles. I was on my way to New Zealand. I was very excited about an opera I was going to create with rock musicians.

Michael came to the airport and told me. Kenny had been dead for over a year.

Michael took Pat and me to lunch. He always did this when I had a stopover in Los Angeles. While we ate, Pat told me it would be our last time together, because she was going to live the rest of her life close to her daughter in Nevada. It didn't occur to either one of us that I could come and visit her.

When people ask me about my sister, I say, "We were never close." Usually that puts an end to the questions. But the questions keep going on inside me.

About a year ago I got a phone call. It was Michael on one phone with Maryann on another. Together they told me that Pat had died.

I asked where and when the funeral would be, already figuring I'd have to borrow money for the flight.

"No funeral," Michael said. "She didn't want one."

He told me her two sons had driven to Nevada to be at her bedside. She'd said good-bye to them, and sent them back to California. She didn't want them waiting around while she died.

"Pat lived her life the way she wanted it," Michael said.

Maryann started talking about a big family gathering a couple of years ago. All Pat's loved ones had come together in Riverside, California, to honor Pat on her birthday. Michael and Maryann had been there. Michael had phoned me in Brownsville, during the party, and had gotten Pat on the phone.

I remember that phone call. I got so excited I didn't realize that I kept talking and talking. Finally Pat stopped me. She said she had to get back to the party. I should have known! All these years and I still didn't know how to talk to my sister.

When Michael called to tell me Pat was dead, my first thought had been how to get the plane fare to the funeral. Then Michael said no funeral. I felt like crying. I wanted to be with Pat's loved ones. I know it's not realistic. I probably wouldn't have known her children. Or their children! But even now I wonder how it might have been if we'd come together.

On the phone Michael said, "Pat had a good life. She lived the way she wanted. Never gave up cigarettes. Had her martinis every night. Right up to the end."

I wondered what murder mystery my sister had been reading at the end. Mystery books were one of the things she and I could talk about when we met over our lunches with Michael.

PART 6

Michael's Tape

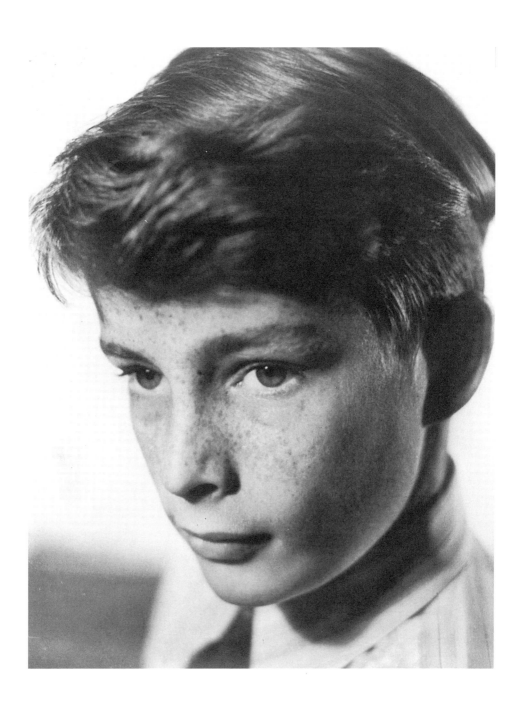

18

Michael's Side of the Story

MICHAEL SENT ME the tape he promised me. Just when I'd about given up hope. I listen. I laugh. I wonder. His story. My story. The story in the photograph albums. Same time, same place, same people, and so different.

Michael's affectionate name for Papa was Elmo. At first the tape sounds like the whole thing's going to be one of Michael's jokes.

Maryann speaks first.

MARYANN, IN TENSE MONOTONE, THE NARRATOR OF A SUSPENSE THRILLER.

> *Michael. Is putting milk back into the refrigerator.*
> *Michael. Is opening the drawer.   Michael. Is getting a spoon with which to eat his cereal. Is closing the drawer. Is dipping his spoon into the cereal!*
> *Today is Tuesday.*
> *Nine o'clock ... seven o'clock! Nine after seven o'clock."*

SOUND OF HER LAUGHTER AS THE RECORDER CLICKS OFF.

RECORDER CLICKS ON.

SOUND OF MICHAEL'S CAR DRIVING IN TRAFFIC ON AN L.A. FREEWAY. MICHAEL, AN ON-THE-SPOT REPORTER IN A MOVIE STUDIO.

> *We're here on the set. Documentary being made. Elmer Clifton. Pioneer motion picture director.*
> *No expense has been spared doing the research to make sure this documentary is as factual as it can possibly be.*

We're ready to begin!
Lights.
Camera.
Roll 'em.
ACTION!

ELMER CLIFTON

    Once upon a time. There was a young man. Living in Canada. He didn't realize it, but his life was touched…

    …By the Potato Famine! Because the Potato Famine was a significant factor in our lives.

    The Potato Famine in Ireland prompted our mother's family migration. From County Clare in Ireland to Brooklyn, New York.

    The Potato Famine on the Isle of Guernsey, between France and England, prompted Elmer Clifton's family to migrate to Quebec, Canada. Where Elmer grew up. Elmer Clifton was actually not his name. Elmer Clifton is a stage name. I've run into a lot of traffic.

RECORDER CLICKS OFF.

MICHAEL SAYS PAPA grew up in Quebec. This photo says Los Angeles. On the back it says: *Elmer Clifton Owens.*

E·A·&·F·J·STAFFLIN

2910 MICHIGAN AVE.
LOS ANGELES, CAL.

Papa's mother with one of her husbands. According to Aunt Grace she had five husbands. Was this one named Owens? Did Papa know his own father?

RECORDER CLICKS ON:

Well, I'm back, the traffic has eased up a little and I'm ... Anyway ... Elmo was a THESPIAN. And he appeared in French Canadian plays in Quebec. One of them was reasonably successful and they were asked to play Chicago.

And so he entered the United States. And this play was quite successful. And he was quite successful. And he was asked to appear in a play in New York City.

So ... Instead of going back to Canada when the run ended in Chicago, he went to New York. By then he was an illegal immigrant.

And he was quite successful in New York. And…

…Took an interest in the silent movie business which was just getting started.

And he was with a company, an actor, but also starting to direct.

He was working at the Vitagraph Studios in Manhattan when he met mother.

Papa as Crazy Joe in Southern Terror

Clara Bow, unknown man, Papa, Mama

Mother's family was fairly well-to-do. Her uncle was a banker in Manhattan. And... When mother got out of high school, she got a job as some sort of teller, or clerk, or something in her uncle's bank. And she and her uncle used to commute to Manhattan together. By car. Or trolley. I don't know. But they went back and forth from Brooklyn to lower Manhattan. And she worked in this bank building with her uncle. But she didn't like banking.

She wanted something more exciting in her life.

Clara Bow and Mama "on the town"

So. During her lunchtime Mother used to wander around and inter-view for other jobs. And she got a job in Vitagraph. But she didn't know how to tell her family. She told her uncle, and they decided they wouldn't tell anyone yet. So. They continued to go together to the bank, and Mama would walk out one of the side entrances, and go to work at Vitagraph Studios.

SOUND OF CAR TURN SIGNAL CLICKING.

RECORDER CLICKS OFF.

MICHAEL'S STORIES DON'T MATCH the stories I heard from Mama. I thought she came from a poor Irish Catholic family in Brooklyn. Her father sounded like a character out of a barroom ballad. Mama would say he'd come home just long enough to produce another offspring. Then off he'd go! Gallivanting around the world.

Mama was the second youngest of twelve. And it seemed like all the children stayed at home or lived close by even when they married.

Except for Mama and her sister, Loretta.

Loretta became a Carmelite nun. She took the name Sister Mary Dorinda. "What a waste," my mother used to say. "Loretta was a beautiful woman. She could have had whatever she wanted."

I thought my aunt becoming a nun was a wonderful, mysterious thing to do. I liked being named Dorinda after her. The only time I ever heard from Sister Mary Dorinda was at my First Holy Communion. She sent me a little white purse just big enough for a prayer book with colored pictures and ruby glass rosary beads.

This photograph came to our house after her death. It was taken on the day she'd come out of the convent to be at her mother's funeral.

RECORDER ON.

So in the course of working at Vitagraph, Mother fell in love with Elmer Clifton.

Who was married to Adele.

And ... Anyway. It became very complicated.

RECORDER OFF.

Adele Clifton

ONCE, A FEW YEARS before Mama's death, I told her how I'd always thought her watch looked so pretty on her wrist. Mama would gain, lose, gain weight over the years, but she always had slender wrists and ankles.

The watch was silver with a black ribbon strap and a silver buckle.

Mama said, "Your father gave it to me. Just before the world trip."

Talking about it made her angry. "He took me into the jewelry store. Put this watch on my wrist. Then picked out a bracelet that cost ten times as much! He had it sent to his first wife! I told him it would make her demand more alimony!"

I've always wondered why my father sent his first wife that bracelet. What did it look like? Maybe silver with jewels. Brightly colored jewels. Round jewels! Round to remind her of the day the two of them played marbles together.

I imagine it as a farewell gift.

His way of saying good-bye.

RECORDER ON.

Pat was born on a ship called Manganui. The captain wanted to name her Manganui Clifton. It wasn't very well received by the rest of the family.

She was born between Australia and New Zealand.

Proud Papa holds Pat in basket

I guess that even at that point Mother and Elmo weren't married. Anyway there was a marriage certificate in some of the paperwork, so eventually they did get married. And... But... It was complicated. Anyway...

PAUSE. TRAFFIC NOISES.

So. Elmo not only had a long-time relationship with D. W. Griffith but also with William Fox, who was the founder of Twentieth Century Fox.

I remember Elmo used to tell a story of a poker game that used to go on. That Bill Fox and other friends of his, successful friends of his, used to play. And in this poker pot there would not only be money, but there would be jewelry. And there would be keys to a car. Or… And one of the things that used to come up in this pot, with some regularity, was a deed to some six hundred acres in a place called Palos Verdes.

And somebody owned it and kept putting it into the pot when they got a chance. And it was somewhat of a negative thing, because no one wanted to win the damn deed.

Nobody wanted this property. So—joke! Six hundred acres in Palos Verdes! And Elmo won it a few times! And lost it.

And it was in 1941. Elmo had won this poker pot. And we had gone out to Palos Verdes. In the big Lincoln convertible. In a family outing. Our goal was to find this property in Palos Verdes.

RECORDER OFF.

SO HERE WE ARE. In Palos Verdes. Michael took this picture of me and Papa and Mama, gazing out at the ocean. We're standing on property that's now worth millions of dollars. What if Papa hadn't gambled it away? What would have happened to us?

But how could Papa be playing poker?

I remember that we had no money in 1941. That was the year I auditioned to play the part of Ginger Rogers as a child. Papa's unemployment checks had run out. I hoped the Ginger Rogers part would bring us lots of money.

Mama made me a costume. I stood while she fitted it on me. She kept the pins in her mouth and I worried about her swallowing them.

Miss Rogers was very particular about who would play her as a little girl. I went back to three auditions to line up in front of the director, producer, casting director. Finally one other girl and myself were chosen to be interviewed by Miss Rogers.

The next day the casting director took both of us to the soundstage where the movie was being shot. Miss Rogers would decide between the two of us.

Her dressing room was up on wheels with stairs like a drawbridge to a fairy castle. When it was my turn to walk up those stairs, I felt like I was entering the presence of a queen.

I went up all by myself. It was a private interview. Miss Rogers wanted it that way. She wanted to talk to me alone.

I knocked on the door. Her beautiful voice called out to me, "Enter."

I stepped inside.

She turned from her dressing table mirror, and greeted me graciously. She stayed seated so her blue eyes were on a level with mine.

I knew I looked pretty in my ballet costume. Mama had worked until after midnight to get it finished. A tight pink satin bodice, then layer after layer of short stiff tutu sticking out. I felt like a real ballerina.

Miss Rogers put her hands on my waist as she spoke. She was so nice, so kind. I forgot all about being self-conscious. I felt like she was really interested in what I had to say.

"Dorinda," she said smiling. "So you are going to be a dancer just like me." She was a ballroom dancer.

"Oh no, Miss Rogers," I carefully explained. "Not like you. I'm going to be a real dancer."

I never knew I'd said the wrong thing until later. I thought everybody knew that ballet was the only real dance. I was happily telling Mama all about the nice talk we'd had when Mama cut me short.

"Why'd you say a thing like that? You ruined your chances!"

She was right. The other girl got the part. Papa never said anything, but I knew I had failed him.

RECORDER ON.

So. 1941. It was a Sunday. And we went picnicking in Palos Verdes. We found a place. We had a beautiful view of the ocean. And we were picnicking on this hillside. And. We noticed that an army truck came by.

And some guys with rifles got out. And started spacing themselves along the peninsula there. Papa went down and talked with them.

It was then that we learned that it was Dec. 7, 1941, and the Japanese had just bombed Pearl Harbor.

The war years were not easy. But... Actually Elmer did pretty well. He made a lot of Navy training films. That was a nice steady income. Very stable. We lived on Glen Green in Beachwood Canyon.

But after the Second World War. He never seemed to get back into... into the mainstream of motion picture making. Can't say why.

I missed a lot in those early years. Just a little kid I guess...

But Elmo was… He had a circle of sort of cronies. Characters. Donald Crisp was one. British actor. They were good friends.

You probably remember Yakima Canute, American Indian stuntman.

And there was a black chauffeur that I remember. Lots of Jewish people. An Irishman. It was nice. I think the diversity was beneficial to me in life.

This menagerie of characters that were our parents' friends. I grew up accustomed to black people.

Like the gal that used to take care of us. The heavyset woman. Forget her name….

RECORDER CLICKS OFF.

HER NAME WAS MARY. I remember she had a rich, full voice. She'd sing about Jesus as she stood barefoot, ironing. Her feet seemed very big to me, and the soles were light like the palms of her hands. She told me she was pastor of her church. I wondered what kind of a church that was.

One day Mama told her she'd have to stop coming, we couldn't pay her anymore. Mary said she'd come for no money. And she did.

RECORDER CLICKS ON WITH MICHAEL SINGING.

Oh, the Cliftons.
The Cliftons.
We got a lot of dough.
We let it rain or snow.
Oh, the Cliftons.
A very very merry lot are we.
Diddle-ee-um. Dum. Dum.

Remember that? That was a few years ago! Anyway. There were a lot of characters at Republic where Elmo made batches of Westerns.

When I was a little kid I used to go out to Corrigan's Ranch where he was making movies… And. I'd hang out. I'd look at the horses. And the cowboys. That was kind of fun.

I don't know if I mentioned the big Christmas we had at Sierra Bonita one year… And the Westerns we used to make on the little porch that was our theater where we had somebody's wooden horses that had little curtains on them to hide our legs. We'd ride in and out on these.

RECORDER OFF.

I'd forgotten those horses! And our Westerns! I loved doing them! Once I was the barmaid—a woman of ill-repute. I still remember most of my song. I can hear myself singing through my nose, belting it out with great gusto.

> *Hard Hearted Hannah,*
> *The vamp from Savannah,*
> *The meanest gal in town…*

> *Rock is hard, but Hannah's heart is*
> *harder. She's a gal that likes to see them*
> *suffer. To torture, to kill them. To*
> *torture and kill them. That's her delight*
> *they say.*

> *And when Hannah sits on your knee,*
> *It's like going through Alaska in your*
> *Beebeedees.*

I just found out it was *B.V.D.s*. All my life I've been singing *Beebeedees*. Our director, the boy next door, told us it was long, woolen underwear.

RECORDER ON.

> *Anyway. Ummm… Mother. I haven't talked much about mother.*
> *What first comes to mind is that she had all these great old sayings:*

> > *'None the worse for wear.'*

> > *'You have a mind like a sieve.'*

> > *'In one ear and out the other.'*

> > *'Handsome is as handsome does.'*

'Six of one, half a dozen of another.'

'He looks like death warmed over.'

'Take it with a grain of salt.'

'It will all come out in the wash.'

'You look like the last six minutes of a misspent life.'

'Blind in one eye, can't see out the other.'

Oh! And then there was…

MICHAEL CHUCKLES.

…there was: 'MONEY, MONEY, MONEY.'
Remember that one?

MICHAEL NARRATES A CLIFTON FAMILY SCENE.

We're all in the living room. The telephone rings. Two off-stage voices
sing out: 'MONEY, MONEY, MONEY.'

RECORDER OFF.

THE MONEY, MONEY, MONEY ritual came from Dr. Litzer's lectures on Science of Mind that Papa and Mama went to every Sunday at the Roosevelt Hotel on Hollywood Boulevard.

I'd come to the Roosevelt after singing Mass at Blessed Sacrament. I'd be first out of the choir loft, down the narrow winding stairs, through the big open double doors of the Catholic cathedral on Sunset Boulevard, to race the five blocks to Dr. Litzer's Science of Mind lecture.

At the entrance, I'd stop. Enter quietly. My shoes making no sound on the lush red carpet as I went across the lobby, through delicate, glass French doors into the lounge, past the book table in the rear with a book Mama and Papa had bought: *Think and Grow Rich.*

I'd sit in the back. I loved being there with Papa and Mama.

And I loved hearing Dr. Litzer. My favorite time was at the very end when we'd all sit quietly with our hands open on our laps. Silence for a minute, then we'd softly sing with our eyes closed:

> *Open my eyes that I may see*
> *Glimpses of truth thou hast for me*
> *Place in my hands the wonderful key*
> *That shall unclasp and set me free.*

I remember imagining the beautiful golden key being placed in my open hand. Sometimes I believed I could feel it there.

I always believed in the MONEY, MONEY, MONEY ritual. My way of performing it was to sing out the word as I ran for the phone.

Papa's way was to repeat the word quietly to the rhythm of his firm, purposeful strides.

Mama's way was to stand by the phone, her hand on the receiver, her eyes pressed tightly closed, whispering the word three times, "Money. Money. Money."

Pat wouldn't do any of this. She just answered the phone.

I don't remember what Michael did.

RECORDER ON. SOUND OF CAR DIRECTION SIGNAL CLICKING.

"I'm driving across town. Coming down Sixth Street. Approaching Sixth and Alexandria. That bring back any memories?"

RECORDER OFF.

SIXTH AND ALEXANDRIA—Rozelle Frey's Dance Studio.

It was a huge, two-story-high room that took up the whole floor above Ralph's Market.

For years, I went all the way across town to Rozelle Frey's studio. The bus fare was a constant problem. Ten cents to get there. Ten cents to get home.

I remember one Saturday morning coming into the kitchen to get the twenty cents from Mama.

"There is no money!" Mama said. "There's no money in this house for anything!"

I couldn't believe it. If only she'd told me earlier, I could have gone bottle hunting at the Hollywood Bowl. Our house on Grace Avenue was only five blocks from the Bowl. I could always find pop bottles there. I'd take them to the little corner grocery store at the bottom of our hill. I'd get more than enough for my bus fare.

But that morning there was no time to go hunting. I had to have a dime to get across town, and a dime to come back home.

I went out on the back porch and opened the pantry cupboard. I don't know what I hoped to find there.

What I did find were several cans of cat food that were for Mama's cat, Little Reddie. Eleven cents a can.

"Mama," I called out. "Can I take two of these cans of cat food back to the grocer?"

"Do what you want," Mama said. "I don't care."

I took two cans, grabbed my dance suitcase, ran down the hill.

I only slowed down and began dragging my feet when I turned the corner and walked sadly into the little grocery store. The owner was standing behind the counter.

"My little kitty died," I said. "Now I have no kitty to eat this cat food. Could you please give me my money back?"

He frowned and gave me a long look. I was afraid he was going to say no. But he pushed the button on the cash register. It clanged open. He gave me the two dimes and the two pennies. He didn't say a word. I thanked him and ran off.

RECORDER ON.

Oh, lots of people had high hopes for our theatrical careers. Yours happened. Mine didn't quite happen. Except. I was always on the fringes. Matty King said to say hello.

MICHAEL CHUCKLES WICKEDLY. RECORDER OFF.

MATTY KING TAUGHT ME tap dancing. I'd come home from my lesson and try to teach Michael and Don White, the boy next door.

I would get excited and shout above the music. "Dance on the balls of your feet! Dance on your balls!"

Years later Michael told me how they had both laughed at me. I told him they'd been cruel not to tell me what I was saying.

RECORDER ON.

'Blind in one eye, can't see out the other.'

Did I mention that one? It's one of the problems of getting as old as I am, I can't remember what I've done and what I haven't done. And. It's difficult.

But the nice thing about senility is you forget you're incontinent.

A WOMAN LAUGHS. MARYANN MUST BE IN THE CAR WITH MICHAEL. HE IS LAUGHING TOO.

Well, perhaps that's it for now. You'd think in eighteen years I would know more than half a tape plus a couple of minutes. But... There was the whole Ida Lupino thing...

But you probably remember all that better than I do. I was preoccupied
with high school by then.
Anyway....

RECORDER OFF.

The year Ida Lupino came into our lives was the year Papa died. But
Michael doesn't talk about that.

RECORDER ON.

Maybe I don't have any other memories. I don't know. But I'll keep the
tape for a few more days.
I don't know how helpful it's been. But. We'll see.
I could make up some stories....

MICHAEL LAUGHS.

Bye.

RECORDER CLICKS OFF FOR THE LAST TIME.

MICHAEL'S STORIES. My stories.
I know we're not making them up. It sounds like he heard most of his
from Papa. And I, from Mama. So who was making them up?
Michael talked about Papa's work. But my question is: why didn't Elmer
Clifton ever make another *Down to the Sea in Ships*? One extraordinary movie
in a lifetime?
Michael says Papa was happy with his work? Was he?

'*Ask me no questions, and I'll tell you no lies.*'

Michael forgot this saying of Mama's.
I can't forget it.
She said it to me too many times.

Elmer Clifton directing a Western at Corrigan's Ranch

PART 7

Dreams Can Come True

19

Wishful Thinking

My Window

A BIRD! SMALL. Fast flying. Here. There. Gone.

Another! Chasing her. A swift swain pursuing his love. Alive with spring.

But it's a false spring. Are there buds peeking out? I hope not. It's a season out of season. Tricking the birds and the bees. Today the warm touch of Spring, tomorrow the icy caress of the heavy-cloaked Father Frost. Father Frost who used to sneak stealthily through the pages of a book I wish I had never read as a child.

Father Frost with icy bone fingers smoothing his deadly sweet, silver frosting over the tiny trusting buds.

Aesop's Fables

Another book I hated as a child! My mind still worries over those stories. Trying to reshape, rewrite the lives of the characters.

THE ANT AND THE GRASSHOPPER

Why is the Busy Ant the hero?

Ant.

I don't want to be that Busy Ant, crawling in the footsteps of its nose-to-the-grindstone neighbor, keeping to the straight and narrow.

Grasshopper of the family Locustidae. *Locusta viridissima* of Europe.

I am the Grasshopper! The merry minstrel! Why does winter put an end to my song, and condemn me to be a dried-up corpse, eternally blowing in the cold, hard wind of reality?

THE TORTOISE AND THE HARE!
I am the Fun-loving Rabbit.
Running the race my way!
Delighting in my harmless devilment!
Secure in my knowledge that
the race is won by the swift,
the fleet, the footloose,
the fancy free!

European Hare (*Lepus timidus*). (½0)

But who do I see?
Ahead of me?
The Trudging Turtle!
Its accordion neck,
protruding, stretching
its dinosaur profile
almost to the finish line!

Snapping Turtle (*Chelydra serpentina*).

Swamp-hare (*Lepus aquaticus*).

But here I come!
Quick as a flash!
I leap over the turtle's humdrum reality,
and win the race!

THE GREEDY FOX
I am The Fox. Not greedy!
But hungry. Brave.
Resourceful.

I squeeze my skinny little
body through the hole in the
farmer's wall.

I eat my fill
of the rich,
sweet, juicy grapes.

Red Fox (*Vulpes fulva*).

And!
Even with my tummy full,
I escape the farmer!

I slip smoothly back through
the hole in the wall!
And run free! Free!

I'm always trying to make these stories come true the way I want them to.

Dreaming up new endings.

20

The Bride on the Billboard

THE BRIDE ON the Billboard dreams.

The sun rises up over the Hollywood hills
to light upon her glowing face.

The face of the virgin bride shining down
on the morning traffic
in Hollywood, California, 1946.

Cadillacs.
Sports Cars.
Old cars and new.

The Hollywood movie-making people
driving by
the Bride on the Billboard.

She calls out to them. SEE ME. SEE ME. They're on their way to their movie-making jobs. SEE ME, she calls. AND MAKE ME A STAR.

> *It's a Barnum and Bailey world.*
> *Just as phony as it can be.*
> *But it wouldn't be make-believe*
> *If you believed in me.*

BELIEVE IN ME, the Bride on the Billboard calls out to me. To me, seventeen years old, as I stand looking up at my eight-foot-high face of the Bride.

BELIEVE IN ME, the Bride calls. BELIEVE IN ME.

And I do believe. I make myself believe. I believe she is me. And that Hollywood will see. Me. And make me a star.

ALL THE WORDS of the promise on my billboard were: "Dreams *can* come true." But, when the photographer mailed me the picture, the whole promise didn't come with it. He couldn't fit the whole thing into the envelope.
So he cut off "*can* come true" and left me with "Dream."

21

The Attack of the Spider

THIS MORNING, BEFORE DAWN, fortified with coffee, I open the door to my window.

Skeleton trees! Silhouetted against the cold grey sky. I imagine a great web stretching between the bony tree branches. Me, caught! In the web! Helpless!

A writer-eating spider tiptoes over its rope bridge. It binds me around and around in its sticky, slimy, silver cocoon. It paralyzes me with its poison words so I won't keep writing *my* words down in this book. The spider gets *its* words from the same dictionaries I use.

I close the door on my window.

I'll wait until daylight.

That spider can't live in the light of day.

BUT NOW, with the door of my window closed, a new hallucination! Butterflies! Trapped in here with me! Flying crazily around and around this little space where I live.

What shall I do?

So they'll not be hurt?

I know what I'll do. I'll turn my computer into a gentle butterfly net. I'll catch the butterflies that are filling my room this morning.

I'll write like a scientist, telling only what I know about them.

A caterpillar goes into a cocoon and comes out a butterfly. It can be scientifically studied. But there are things about the life of caterpillars and butterflies that scientists can't pin down. A butterfly has to be dead to be pinned down.

I'll identify my butterflies precisely, then let them go flying out my window.

I'll keep them alive by only writing what I know about them. Not trying to explain what I *don't* know about them.

explain, [L. explanare to *flatten*]

IN MY FIRST LEADING role I was a collector of butterflies. A girl who grew up living by a swamp. I had to hide my butterflies from my mother. She hated me for causing my father's death. It was my fault because when she was trying to save him from drowning in quicksand, she was overcome with labor pains, had to give birth to me while he sank to his death in the quicksand of the swamp.

The happy ending is my mother finds out that the night he fell into the quicksand, he was on his way home from visiting his mistress. So she stops hating me, and starts hating him.

It's a famous Gene Stratton Porter novel that Hollywood used to make into a movie about every ten years. Mine was 1945.

The film test which won me the part was a scene with the Butterfly Lady. I needed money to pay for school books, so I came to the Butterfly Lady asking her to buy my collection of butterflies. I showed the butterflies to her in a box, all pinned down.

Mel Ferrer was the director of the movie. I was very shy with him. I couldn't tell him how awful I felt when I looked at the beautiful butterflies all flattened out, dead on the end of the pins. But the actress who played the Butterfly Lady knew how I felt.

During our scene, she helped me look starry-eyed over the butterflies I had impaled on pinpoint.

Michael used to say Papa always concentrated on me and my career. But it was Mama. She was the one who always got me ready for auditions. And when I did *Girl of the Limberlost*, it was Mama who tried to coach me in the acting.

In one scene, Mama was trying to get me to cry. She kept saying, "Look at me! Look at me!" Tears rolling down her cheeks.

I couldn't do it. I finally blurted out, "Mama, all my life you've said don't cry, don't cry! And now you expect me to cry!"

The director, Mel Ferrer, had to use drops in my eyes for tears. I was embarrassed. But, even without real tears, I did a good job with the role. *The Hollywood Reporter* said I was a "finished actress." This got to be a joke around our house because I was finished at Columbia. My agent was sure I'd be signed up to a seven-year contract, but I wasn't.

No Sex Appeal

A few months later, I was rehearsing on the stage of the Philharmonic Auditorium. I had a small part in *The Three Musketeers* for Edwin Lester Productions.

WARRIORS AND FAIR MAIDENS—in "The Three Musketeers," Monday at the Philharmonic Aud. Left to right, Earle MacVeigh, Dorinda Clifton, John Tylers, Gwen Verdon, Richards Charles, H. Calvin.

During a break in rehearsal, Edwin Lester came up to me while I was stretched out, lying flat across three wooden chairs, trying to rest.

He told me that the night before, at a party at the house of Harry Cohn, head of Columbia Studios, he'd asked Cohn why Columbia hadn't picked up the option on my contract.

Harry Cohn said that I had no sex appeal.

Edwin Lester was trying to help me. But what could I do? How do you make yourself have sex appeal?

I was still saving my first kiss for my first and only love.

22

The Bride on the Billboard Appears

She was The Bride
on the Billboard.

The star of *The Girl of the
Limberlost.*

And so she was elected one
of the six Ephibians
at Hollywood High.

She and Charlotte Solomon,
her one friend in high school,
laughed about this.

"Everyone knew your name on the ballot," Charlotte told her. "But nobody knows you."

An Ephibian had to have the highest grades in her class—which she had.

An Ephibian had to be one of the most popular seniors in her class—which she wasn't.

She and Charlotte went to one party—planned by the school. At the party, she didn't want anyone to know she didn't have a boyfriend.

Some enchanted evening
You may see a stranger
Across a crowded room.

So, weaving through the crowd, she kept her eyes fixed on an imaginary boyfriend as she hurried to him.

Then fly to his side,
And make him your own

She pictured her imaginary stranger and herself leaving the party together. Driving into the starry night in his hopped-up powder-blue Model A Ford.

Or all through your life
You may dream alone.

She learned the ways of love through books, songs, movies. She watched Lena Horne's secretive smile, teeth clenched as she sings, relishing each word:

Love can be a moment's magic.
Love can be a flame.

Sitting next to her sister in the movie theater, she saw Lena Horne's nostrils flare out as she sang.

"What's wrong with her nose?" she whispered to Pat.

"Nothing," Pat hissed back. "She's *sexy*." Pat hated people talking in movies.

Love is hardly ever, ever the same.

She couldn't make her nose like Lena Horne's, but she could make her voice like Lauren Bacall talking to Humphrey Bogart at the door of her bedroom.

If you want anything, just whistle.

She practiced the deep, throaty voice. But when she tried it out on people, they thought she had a cold. Her brother called her Gravel Gertie, the Dick Tracy cartoon character.

> *The thing that's known as romance*
> *Is wonderful, wonderful*
> *In every way,*
> *So they tell me.*

Once she played SPIN THE BOTTLE. The other kids were older than she, Pat's friends. Maybe they let her play so she wouldn't tell Mama what they were doing. They sat in a circle with the bottle spinning in the middle. When it stopped, whoever the neck pointed at would be kissed.

She remembered the spinning bottle, but not the kisses. Maybe the bottle never stopped to point at her.

A Date in Fifth Grade

At St. Ambrose she went on a double-date. They met at the school playground, so Papa and Mama never knew about it. The four of them walked to the Monica Theater on Santa Monica Boulevard. Sitting in the theater, she didn't let the boy she was with hold her hand, because Tommy Jordan, the boy she really wanted to be with, was sitting behind them.

She would have let Tommy Jordan hold her hand. Tommy Jordan wrote notes and hid them for her to find under the wastepaper basket in class. But he was too shy to ask her for a date.

Maybe he would have gotten up his nerve, but a few months later her family moved again. This time to the Sierra Bonita house.

So she left St. Ambrose, and didn't see Tommy Jordan for three years.

When she started at her new school, Blessed Sacrament, she told her mother: "I'm a sixth grader now, I'll be going on dates."

Her mother said, "Oh you will, will you?" Her mother made it sound like it wasn't going to happen.

Her mother was right. She didn't go on dates. But she didn't feel bad because at Blessed Sacrament just girls who were known to be wild went on dates.

When her class graduated, she was the only one who didn't go on to Catholic high school. It cost too much money. She went to Hollywood High. This was hard because she didn't come with a group of friends. She did connect in with Charlotte Solomon, but Charlotte didn't have any friends either. So it was just the two of them. No boyfriends.

Tommy Jordan

Tommy Jordan went to Hollywood High, too. Once he stopped her when she was hurrying across the Quad. She hadn't seen him since St. Ambrose. She didn't have time to talk, she was on her way to the bus stop to go to her dancing lesson. Maybe he thought she didn't want to talk. Soon after that she was gone from Hollywood High for a semester. She went to Chicago with *The Waltz King*. A light opera.

When she came back she had to go to a private school. It was a kind of fraud. She paid a tuition fee and the school gave her a certificate saying she'd been attending their school for the whole semester, while most of that time she and her mother had been on the road with *The Waltz King*.

She didn't see Tommy Jordan when she got back to Hollywood High. He probably saw her. Maybe he thought she was dating movie stars.

One Date in High School

It was with a boy who kept hanging around Charlotte and her. One day he asked her out for his birthday. She and Charlotte were both surprised. They'd thought it was Charlotte he liked.

Charlotte told her to go. Charlotte said she didn't care.

His mother called her mother. The date ended up to be in a nightclub on the Sunset Strip.

His mother and three of his aunts came, too. They had the nightclub photographer take their picture around the table. They had her sign her name on the photograph as *The Girl of the Limberlost*. She hated it. Maybe the boy did, too. He never spoke to her after that.

She told Charlotte how awful it had been, but still, things were never the same between them after that date.

Wanted by the Police

The day she posed for the bride on the billboard, she had to leave school early. She told her teacher, Miss Theap, that she had been chosen to be the model for a billboard. Miss Theap let her out of her fourth period dance class. Charlotte signed her name on the roll sheet for fifth period study hall. So off she went at eleven o'clock. It was the first time she'd ever ditched school.

A few days later, she knew she hadn't gotten away with it. A student messenger came to take her to the Vice Principal.

When she walked into the office, everybody in the room stared at her. The Vice Principal, no smile on her face, Miss Theap, who looked more nervous than usual, and a policeman and a policewoman. The policewoman said she'd committed a crime.

Guilty Although Proven Innocent

Even today I can't figure out how it happened. But it did. At the same time I was at the photography studio, sitting before the camera, wearing a bridal gown with a row of clothespins in the back pinching it tight, with lights coming at me from every direction, while I was there, another Hollywood High School girl was walking down Hollywood Boulevard and into Nancy's Dress Shop. She tried on several dresses, picked out the most expensive one, and paid for it with a check which she signed Dorinda Clifton.

The policeman and the policewoman said it was me.

I knew it wasn't. But I felt guilty. It was like the time when I was a little girl and Mama accused me of stealing her green ring. It was so easy for me to feel guilty.

Miss Theap spoke up in her high shrill voice, "Nonsense! Dorinda was in my fourth period class that day!"

Miss Theap

She taught forty years at Hollywood High. For gym classes, she wore shorts down to her bony knees. For dance classes, she changed into a flowing Grecian costume.

Her English accent was real. But the girls made it sound ridiculous when they imitated her in the locker room. They also mocked the way she talked to people, her scrawny neck thrusting her sharp chin up in the air, her eyes focused off into space. Poor skinny old scarecrow Miss Theap was a school joke.

I never made fun of her, but I felt guilty when she called me her friend. The only reason I was nice to her was because she let me take over her dance class. I created dances with the girls in class, and then saw my work performed on the big stage. Thanks to Miss Theap, I was teaching myself to be a choreographer.

Once she took me into her office. Closed and locked the door. And then she started whispering. I didn't know why. She was so nervous and embarrassed she could hardly get the words out. I could barely understand what she was trying to tell me.

Finally I realized she desperately wanted me to know how to defend myself if a man grabbed me. She jerked up her knee, demonstrating how it would cripple him.

Both of us were excruciatingly embarrassed.

She thought we were kindred souls. Vestal maidens keeping alive the flame of pure dance.

> **maiden, 1.** Young unmarried woman, virginal, chaste. **2.** Scotch Maiden, a machine for beheading, introduced into Scotland by the Regent Morton who died by its axe 1681.

> *The rude old guillotine of Scotland*
> *called the Maiden.*
> Macaulay: *Hist. Eng.*

A couple of years after I graduated, Miss Theap phoned me. She'd gotten my number from the school records. She had finally been forced to retire. She asked me to come see her.

She lived alone. We sat on the stiff couch facing the false fireplace with its feeble gas flames licking at the non-burnable logs. She explained that she couldn't have a dog, a cat, even a canary. She was allergic to everything.

"I thought we'd be informal," she said.

The coffee table was loaded with overlapping doilies, plates, saucers, a cut glass vase with a rose. And a plate with the imported English tea biscuits she always kept on her desk in her office. They came in a tin box with a painting of Westminster Abbey.

The girls had made fun of these dry cookies. The minute you walked into her office, she'd laugh self-consciously and thrust them at you.

The two of us did our best to talk. She told me how she hadn't wanted to stop teaching at Hollywood High. When I stood up to leave, she said she'd asked me to come for a special reason.

She took me into the dining room. To an antique cupboard with sparkling cut-glass dishes crowded onto the shelves. She opened the wobbly glass doors and asked me to choose what I wanted. She laughed and said she wasn't planning to die for a long time, but she wanted to give away her collection to her friends now.

I felt terrible. Didn't she have any real friends to give her treasures to?

I chose six little salt dishes. She insisted I choose something more. I picked out a delicate cut-glass bowl.

I wish I could say I have them still. One of my sons broke the bowl. Maybe I was glad. Every time I looked at that bowl, I'd feel guilty because I'd promised Miss Theap I'd come have tea with her again, and I never did.

When I divorced my first husband, I left everything behind me, including the six little salt dishes.

I wonder how long Miss Theap lived. What happened to her when she had given away her last precious cut-glass piece? Did she just decide to die?

We should have all come to her funeral. All the ones she'd given her cut-glass treasures to.

One by one, we should have stood up in front of everybody at the funeral. Like Sister Mary Joseph's second graders doing SHOW AND TELL, lifting high the fragile glass love gifts.

"Look," we'd say, as the cut-glass diamonds caught the light streaming through the stained-glass windows. "Look what Miss Theap wanted us to have."

A Dream in the Night

A woman tells me that while she was traveling in a foreign country she saw Miss Theap.

I say, "Tell me! How is she? I've just been writing about her in my book!"

The woman describes a beautiful beach, clean, white sand sloping down to gentle waves on a lake shining with soft warm sunshine.

The woman says, "Miss Theap had spread out her beach towel and was sitting in a beach chair under her umbrella. Two half-grown puppies were playing together beside her."

I asked what kind. In the dream I didn't even think about her allergies.

"I don't know what kind," the woman said. "Just two happy tumbling dust-mop puppies."

23

The Soldier

I WAS HANDING the soldier his roll and butter when he asked if he could walk me home.

I was so surprised, I blurted out, "I don't do that sort of thing!" I felt so stupid! Why did I say that? But the soldier laughed. He thought I was kidding.

It was Sunday morning in the Hollywood High School cafeteria, New Year's Day, 1946. Soldiers were allowed to sleep in the boys' gym Saturday nights. On Sunday morning, the high school seniors served them breakfast.

I was a senior, but I'd never even thought about serving breakfast to the soldiers. They always had more girls than they needed, but this was the morning after New Year's Eve. Nobody wanted to sign up.

I signed up. I didn't go on dates. I thought it would be fun.

The dress I was wearing that morning was wool, emerald green. It made my eyes green. I felt beautiful with him looking at me.

He walked me home, along Hollywood Boulevard, laughing and singing to me.

He asked me if I sang. I said I'd been in the choir at Blessed Sacrament. I started telling him about Mr. Biggs, our famous organist.

He started to laugh. I thought he was laughing at me talking about church. But he was pointing at the five-and-ten-cent stores, two of them standing side by side on Hollywood Boulevard. Woolworth's and Kress, both selling the same things.

It *was* funny! I laughed with him, and forgot all about Blessed Sacrament.

I was glad he kept singing, because I couldn't think of anything to say. As we crossed Hollywood Boulevard and started up Whitley, past the Van de Kamp's bakery, I thought I might say something about the bran muffins with pineapple in them I'd buy on my way to ballet lessons. I liked doughnuts better, but they didn't last until dinner. Mama gave me the bus fare, but the bran muffins came from finding bottles with deposits on them.

I thought of telling him about how Pat and I would pick up bottles at the Hollywood Bowl. Once a month, on Saturday, before dawn, when it was still dark, the two of us, wearing dark clothes, would come down from Whitley Terrace on the Hollywood Bowl side, cross over Highland Avenue, and up the trail through the sagebrush keeping a ridge between us and the Bowl until we'd reached the top. From there, we'd sneak into the Bowl, and start walking back and forth along the rows of seats. We'd be there before the crew came to clean up from the night before. It was barely light enough to see the bottles. We each had a gunnysack that we'd load with as many as we could carry. I couldn't carry as much as Pat. She was big for her age, an athlete. If somebody saw us, we'd have to drop our gunnysacks and run. Pat hated to leave the bottles behind. Once when we had to drop them and run, I heard Pat sobbing as we ran along the trail.

Walking with the soldier up Whitley Avenue, I composed this whole story in my head, but then decided it wouldn't be that interesting to him.

When we reached the house, Papa welcomed us at the door. And so did Mama! It was crazy! Maybe it was the uniform.

> *It's a Barnum and Bailey world.*
> *Just as crazy as it could be.*

Papa invited the handsome soldier to come on our Sunday drive!

And it was fun! Singing songs and laughing with the top down, the sun shining, the wind blowing, Papa in the driver's seat, taking us all for a ride in his wine-colored Lincoln convertible.

> *But it wouldn't be make-believe,*
> *If you believed in me.*

When we came home, the soldier asked if he could take me out to dinner. They said yes! I couldn't believe it. The next thing I knew, I was walking out of the house alone with a handsome stranger I'd just met that morning.

> It's a honky-tonk parade.
> It's a melody played in the penny
> arcade.

We walked side by side along Hollywood Boulevard. Ate dinner in a little nightclub on Vine Street. I'd never known people ate in night clubs. A band played. The singer with the band was Frankie Laine, singing "Black Lace."

> Oh, Lady, beware.
> It's so easy to tear
> Lace. Black Lace.

We walked along Hollywood Boulevard all the way to Brown's Ice Cream Parlor. I'd never been inside. I'd looked in the windows at the little marble-topped tables and fancy wrought-iron chairs. Brown's Hot Fudge Sundaes were famous. But expensive.

He asked me if I wanted one. I said no. We'd had cheesecake for dessert.

But while my lips were saying no, my eyes must have been saying yes. He laughed and took me inside.

A Brown's Hot Fudge Sundae was not big. Just exquisite. Smooth, rich vanilla ice cream with real whipped cream and sliced almonds in a silver pedestal dish on a white saucer with a paper lace doily and a macaroon cookie. The hot fudge came in a small brown ceramic pitcher. You poured just enough over the top of the ice cream for a few bites. Then enough for a few more bites. That way you kept having the magic of the hot and the cold temperatures together. And it wasn't just hot syrup, but real fudge melted.

So much to eat, and yet I didn't feel stuffed. Maybe because of all the walking.

When we got to the house, I could see Papa and Mama through the living-room window.

I thought we would go inside, but he took me on up the Grace Avenue hill.

That's when I knew he was going to kiss me. But I didn't know how I felt about it.

It was a beautiful clear night. The lights of the city were sparkling before us. I was completely happy walking with the soldier, but I was also nervous.

It didn't seem like the right time for the kiss. It was still too early in our story. I kept walking too fast for him. And I couldn't stop the words from tumbling out of my mouth.

We came to the steep Whitley Avenue hill. I told him about Richard Randal, the ninth grader in Blessed Sacrament, who was killed when he and two other boys dared each other to ride their bikes down the Whitley Avenue hill.

Talking faster and faster, I told him how I'd been a seventh grader, singing in the choir at Richard Randal's funeral, going up the winding stairs to the choir loft, looking down at the whole school gathered for the funeral, with sunlight coming through the stained-glass windows.

The soldier stopped our walking at the top of the steep hill. I thought it was because he was so interested in what I was saying about Richard Randal.

Richard had been one of the big boys who stood on the second-story school balcony, and chose what record to put on for all the classes to march into their rooms from the playground. After placing the needle on the record, the boys would leave the balcony to join their class while the marching music kept playing.

One morning, the record was extra loud. Blaring so loudly it reached into the apartment houses surrounding the school. Reached into cars going by on Sunset Boulevard. A marching song for Blessed Sacrament School!

> *I'm a rambling wreck*
> *from Georgia Tech,*
> *and a hell of an engineer.*
> *A hell of a,*
> *hell of a,*

hell of a,
hell of a,
hell of an engineer.

It seemed to go on and on and on forever before the boys could run back up to the balcony and turn it off. The nuns didn't believe that it had been an accident.

The soldier was smiling. I thought it was because of the story I was telling him, "For months, all we kids had to do was hum that tune and we'd burst out laughing. And then Richard Randal, who had been such a funny boy, was dead."

The soldier put his finger to my lips. I felt like I was floating, that he'd cast a spell over me.

Once in a Movie

I had seen the beautiful woman let a rose drop from her hand to the ground while the man she would love forever was kissing her. The violins played. The scene slowly faded out. It was such a romantic movie.

And now, at the top of Whitley Avenue hill, I was the woman being kissed.

While he pressed his lips to mine, I remembered the scene in the movie. I decided to drop what I was holding in my hand.

Unfortunately, it wasn't a light flower floating to the earth. It was my heavy purse that landed with a clump.

He jumped back. He thought someone was there.

I was embarrassed.

I didn't tell him about the scene in the movie.

24

The Bride

With pure white slices of bread.
With pure white virgin veil.
With words floating in the sky.

All over the USA. And in Europe. Words in different
languages. But all with the same promise.

Dreams Can Come True

The soldier, the first man to kiss her, becomes the man whose bride she's promised to be. He writes that her smiling face has been shining down at him from billboards everywhere he goes. France. Switzerland. Germany.

He is the man of her dreams come true. He's filled her with stories of himself: a paratrooper leaping from airplanes, landing on snow-covered mountains, skiing behind enemy lines!

And now a translator! He sends photographs of himself sitting with generals and diplomats, creating the Marshall Plan, deciding the fate of Europe. He's tall, blue eyes, she wishes he didn't have a mustache, but he's her dream come true.

For a whole year his letters come to her. And a magazine with big photographs of castles along the Rhine. "My castles," he writes. "I'll take you to them on our honeymoon."

He is a magician conjuring up visions of the fairytale kingdom he will bring her to as his bride.

> **magician,** One skilled in magic; one who practices the black art; a sorcerer, enchanter.

She writes that as soon as she becomes a big Hollywood star for her father, she can be his bride.

> *I walk alone,*
> *I don't mind being lonely,*
> *When my heart tells me you*
> *Are lonely too.*

He never said he would walk alone while they were apart. She just knows he will.

After dinner, whenever she can, she retraces the steps they had taken together around the hill. Nobody asks why she walks every night. Pat might have been curious, but Pat wasn't part of the family anymore.

Every month, because they met on the first day of the month, a big box of flowers comes to the house.

The first box is filled with red roses. The second is a variety of blossoms. The third box isn't quite filled to the brim.

Her mother comments that each month the boxes stay the same size but the bouquets are more scraggly, left-over looking. Her mother says they should complain to the florist.

In his letters, he asks if the flowers have come, and she writes back something poetic. She knows the truth would disappoint him.

She spends hours writing and rewriting her letters to him.

My Love, she writes. When I am famous, I can be six months your wife in Europe, six months the movie star for Papa.

He sends her picture books of places where they will live in Europe.

> *I walk alone*
> *They ask me why*
> *And I tell them I'd rather.*
> *There are dreams I must gather.*

All her happiness is in the dreaming, the waiting, the solitary evening walks around the hill with her phantom lover.

Then suddenly a telegram. He has a chance to hitchhike a flight. He'll be arriving from Europe in a week for a twenty-four-hour stopover.

She isn't ready for him! She is afraid he is going to ask her to marry him and go back to Europe with him.

She can't do that to her father. She can't marry until she becomes a star. And also she's right in the middle of rehearsing THE THREE MUSKETEERS!

In his letter, he asks if he can stay at her house. She tells Mama that's the way people do it in Europe. But Mama makes Papa get him a hotel room that he'll have to pay for. Papa reserves a room in an old hotel at the bottom of the Grace Avenue hill on Cahuenga Boulevard.

I COULD SEE Cahuenga Boulevard when I looked out my bedroom window. But not the hotel. The old hotel was hidden by the big palm branches that spread all the way to the flat roof of our front porch.

When Pat was still living with us, rats had been using those palm branches as bridges to run along and get into the upstairs of our house. They made nests inside the walls of Pat's bedroom.

Mama bought a box of rat poison that said the rats would eat the poison, then leave the house to go searching for water. The rats were supposed to die outside. Our rats died inside our walls.

Each day the smell got worse. We'd go along smelling the walls inch by inch, then cut holes where it seemed really bad. But we never did find the dead rats. Pat tried pouring perfume into the holes and that made the smell worse. Maybe that's when I stopped liking perfume.

The Bride's Perfume

At Christmas, he sent her perfume from Paris. It was called Je Reviens, which she knew meant either "I return" or "I will return." She knew this because she was studying French. She started with night classes at Hollywood High. Her teacher was Madame Lodine. But she wanted to learn faster, so she went to Madame Lodine's house for private lessons.

It was a strange dark house on Franklin Avenue, designed by Frank Lloyd Wright. The outside wall rose up two stories from the sidewalk with no windows. Cement with Egyptian-looking carvings. You had to enter through a narrow opening like into a tomb, then take a sharp right up steep steps inside a tunnel to the heavy front door. She went once a week.

She was Madame Lodine's favorite pupil. "You have a tongue for the French. The ear for the accent."

She loved learning French. Each time she wrote the soldier, she'd add more and more French phrases. And he'd end his letters with French love phrases.

But when he came back, she was too shy to try to speak with him.

The Hotel

The old hotel on Cahuenga rose up six stories high and curved with the curve of the street. The outside was all brown brick.

The lobby inside felt all brown, too, with heavy wood paneling. She expected to see people in the lobby. But no one was there. No one at the desk. She sat down on a brown leather couch. She thought she was going to wait for him in the lobby.

But he said to come up and help him pack. And then he said something in French. She didn't know what he'd said, but she told him she liked to hear his German accent with his French. That was the wrong thing to say. He said he had no accent.

They were alone in the elevator. He kissed her all the way up to the fourth floor. She knew he was going to make love to her.

The first thing she saw when she walked into the room was a sink in the corner with a strip of brown rust stain around the drain.

She made herself imagine that the sink was filled with the red roses that had come in the first box.

She said, "I wish you could have seen the first roses. They were so..."

He put his finger to her lips. She was talking too loud. Someone might hear. She wasn't supposed to be in his room.

She sat down on the bed. A puff of old perfume rose up.

He hung his pants over the back of a wooden chair to keep the crease.

She lay back on the bed. The ceiling had a brown stain in the corner. The sink on the next floor must have leaked at one time.

She thought he would take off her dress. But it was just her underpants.

> *Love can be a moment's magic.*
> *Love can be a flame.*

She'd thought there would be pain. And blood. There was pain, but no blood.

> *Love is hardly ever ever the same.*

The phone beside the bed rang. She heard him say that she was downstairs in the lobby. He said that he'd just come upstairs that minute to get his bags.

When he hung up, he said it had been her father.

> *Love pledged in September,*
> *May be dead in December.*
> *You may not even remember*
> *It came.*

On his way back to Europe he stopped in New York. There he saw *The Girl of the Limberlost*.

He didn't like it. "That isn't you," he wrote to her.

THIS WAS THE PICTURE he liked of her. He kept it on his desk at work where everyone could see it.

maiden, 3. An animal or a thing that is young, new, inexperienced, untried, not yet touched, handled, or employed for any purpose.

He wrote her one last letter when he got back to Europe. It was almost a poem. He described a dream he'd had of the two of them meeting again years later.

But, dearest Dorinda, he wrote, even if we never meet again, you will always be the love of my life.

She burned his letters and photographs in the backyard incinerator. She never told anybody what had happened. Even when she thought she was pregnant.

Her skin started breaking out. Her mother said, "I thought you'd grown out of pimples." She told her mother she'd been eating too much chocolate.

The Bride Comes Down

In this snapshot, Mama is wearing a big hat. I'm standing with her. I don't know why the billboard came out crooked. The telephone poles look strange, too. Maybe Papa didn't know he was holding the camera wrong.

I was the bride on the billboard for six weeks. Then workmen, standing on hanging planks, wielding big brushes, pasted over my smiling face and my DREAMS CAN COME TRUE with a section by section image of a dark-chocolate Hostess Cupcake broken in half to expose its pure white frosting inside.

What It Means to Be a Woman

A few years before Mama died, I told her how when I first had intercourse, I didn't bleed. I said I'd always wondered if that meant I'd been abused as a child.

"There's lots of reasons girls don't bleed," Mama said. "Like horseback riding."

That ended the discussion. Mama didn't talk about such things. She never told Pat nor me about the facts of life. Neither did the nuns at school. The first time I knew about menstruation was when it happened to me. I was reading a book and suddenly I was bleeding. I didn't know what was wrong. I ran to mother. She told me to stop being so melodramatic.

"That's just what it means to be a woman," she said.

25

The Wild West

I CONCENTRATED ALL my energy and my thoughts on my work. *The Three Musketeers* opened. We played the Los Angeles Philharmonic for two weeks, then went to San Francisco for two weeks.

Gwen Verdon was one of the dancers. She was still in the chorus. This was before she became a star on Broadway. She and two others needed a fourth to pay for a penthouse on top of a hotel near Union Square. I knew they'd tried everybody else in the show before asking me, but that didn't spoil it for me.

Our penthouse was the gathering place for the whole cast. Lots of music, eating, drinking, far into the night. I felt it was the beginning of my new life. We rented records from a music store. All kinds of music. I loved that I could dance on and on, and everybody else kept doing what they wanted to do. I didn't think they were watching me.

A couple of years later I worked with Gwen Verdon on a Gene Kelly movie. She told me that my roommates had been worried about my dancing. She said I'd exhaust myself and then sit in the open window staring out. They were afraid I was thinking of letting myself fall to the sidewalk, ten stories down.

I remember sitting in that open window. I know I wasn't consciously thinking of falling. I was just letting the music sink into me as I looked out over the lights of San Francisco.

Far From Foolproof

When I came home, my agent called, excited, because the Hopalong Cassidy company wanted me to do a second Western with them. He told me that this was very unusual. The Hopalong people never used the same leading lady twice, but they'd liked me so much in the first movie I'd done for them, they wanted me again. What made it extra special for me was we would be shooting ten days on location.

The first movie I'd made with them was called *The Marauders*. Bandits had trapped me and my mother inside our church. My father had been the

pastor. They'd killed him to get the oil "worth a fortune in gold" underneath the church. Like most Westerns, the plot was far from foolproof.

One of the big dramatic moments in the movie started with the sound of a gun shot! Then the death cry of a villain! Then the sound of his body crashing through the ceiling of the church. At that point, the prop man threw a sawdust dummy down from the catwalk. It came plunging down and crashed through the floor of the church.

The script called for me to run up to the edge of the hole in the floor, peer down, and say: "Who was that?"

The line struck me as funny. In the rehearsal, I burst out laughing as I tried to explain why it was such an outlandish thing to say in the circumstances. Nobody else saw it that way, but they enjoyed my laughter. The director just slowly shook his head at me. It was fun working for the Hopalong people.

And now I'd be making a second movie with the same people! I was ready to go. My costumes all fitted. Script memorized.

Then, the week before we were to begin shooting, my face started to break out really bad. I'd had trouble with pimples when I was younger, but nothing like this.

The Hopalong people weren't worried. The make-up man said he could take care of me. The cameraman said, no problem. But then, the Saturday before the Monday we were all going to leave for location, they called me into their office.

Papa dropped me off at the studio gate. It was the independent studio on Santa Monica Boulevard. Papa told me to call when I was done, and he'd come pick me up.

The secretary sent me right into the producer's office. Everybody was there waiting for me. They all looked so sad.

The producer said, Dorinda, we've had to replace you.

I was so surprised that I didn't have time to hide my feelings.

It's the insurance company, he said. They won't insure us with you. They're afraid you might get skin poisoning and sue the company.

The actress who would do my part was there. She looked sorry for me, too. All I could do was get out of there as quickly as possible. I remember I thanked them. I think I even smiled and wished them good luck.

I didn't want to phone Papa from the studio.
I walked out the studio gate.
I waited for the signal on Santa Monica Boulevard.
I crossed the street.

The Phone Booth

I was crying. I closed myself inside a glass telephone booth on the corner of an old, abandoned gas station that was cluttered with junk, overgrown with weeds.

I was in that booth a long time, but no one else came. I dialed wrong and lost my dime. That's when big sobs started pouring out of me.

I found another dime at the bottom of my purse.

When Papa answered, I asked him to come get me.

He said why?

I said I lost the part.

I hung up and then I stayed closed inside the booth because I couldn't stop crying.

I wouldn't look at my reflection in the glass.

I used up all my tissues blowing my nose and scraping away at the layers of make-up that I'd applied so carefully to cover the pimples.

Bucking Bronco.

26

On the Road

MY SKIN MIGHT not have gotten so bad if it hadn't been for a certain black wool hat. It was part of one of my costumes in *The Three Musketeers*.

A black wool hat shaped sort of like an aviator's cap, hugging my cheeks and tight around my chin and neck. My skin couldn't breathe. I knew the black wool was rubbing against my skin, making it worse, but I didn't care because it was hiding the mess.

I also tried to cover the pimples by piling on the makeup. We dancers did our own makeup. We sat lined up side by side every night in front of the long dressing-table mirrors. The other girls were horrified when they saw what I was doing.

Before putting on the greasepaint, I'd squeeze out the pimples to get rid of the white bumps.

Then I'd pile on the makeup to hide the open sores. I put on a dab of medicine before the greasepaint. The medicine burned, so I figured that was taking care of it.

The Healer

Mama learned about him at her writer's group. She must have told the members about her daughter's pimples. One of them gave her this man's phone number. He wasn't a real doctor, but he had healed the writer who gave Mama his name.

Mama called him up and made an appointment for me. It was just before I was going to leave town with the Edwin Lester *Song of Norway* light opera. I thought I'd be seeing him at an office building, but the address was the apartment house where he lived.

I vaguely remember that he was tall and handsome. But what I clearly remember are the photographs he showed me. Pictures of crippled people sitting in the driver's seat of cars, able to drive because of the mechanism this man had created for them. He was proud of what he had done.

He told me my skin would heal. He had me lie down on a flat couch. He shone a warm red light on me. The red light was shining on my face and naked breasts because the pimples were on my chest, too.

He wrote down the name of a vegetable soap. Gave me a note to the pharmacist at the corner drugstore. It was for a quart jar of pure lanolin. He told me to be a vegetarian. And to drink alfalfa tea.

I toured nine months with *Song of Norway*. I loved the music. It was Grieg. The last big dance number was a complete ballet that was originally done in New York by the Ballet Russe.

Normally I wouldn't have taken the job which was just being in the corps de ballet and also doing a small acting part. But the way my skin looked, my agent and my parents were glad to see me leave Hollywood. Fortunately, I didn't know that they didn't expect my skin to heal without scars. They thought that I wouldn't be any good for films anymore.

But I believed that the lanolin, and the rest of the cure would heal me.

I liked being known as a vegetarian. We'd come into a city. I'd go with the rest of the dancers to some famous steak house one of them had discovered. When they ordered their huge platters of meat, I'd ask for the mushrooms on toast. These places always had mushrooms a la carte. It never occurred to me that I was getting all the grease with the mushrooms. I loved mushrooms, and I never did care all that much for meat.

I used the soap and the lanolin. The only thing I could not keep up was the alfalfa tea.

I drank it only once. Opening night at the Los Angeles Philharmonic Auditorium. Just before showtime. I made myself a very strong cup of alfalfa tea. It smelled just like a barn, but I drank it all down.

Later, on stage, during the last big ballet number, I began to perspire. I smelled like a whole barn full of alfalfa hay. As the others went leaping by me, I heard whispers: "Mooo. Moooo."

The smell of alfalfa hay never came out of that ballet costume. As we toured the country, every once in a while someone would dance by me murmuring: "MOOOOO. MOOOOOOOO."

Unwed Mothers

cra′dle (krā′d′l), *n*. [AS. *cradel, cradol;* akin to OHG. *kratto*, G. dial. *kratte* basket, Skr. *grantha* a knot. Cf. CART.] **1. a** A bed or cot for a baby, usually oscillating on rockers or swinging on pivots; hence, the place of origin or where anything is nurtured or protected in the earliest period of existence; as, a *cradle* of crime; the *cradle* of liberty. **b** A kind of basket, frame, or network, in which American Indians bind an infant.

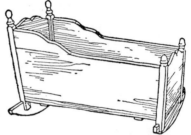

One form of Cradle, **1.** From an 18th-century example.

My periods were so irregular, there was a chance that I wasn't pregnant even though I had missed two.

I decided to wait four months. I figured if I was pregnant, I'd be showing by then.

If I had confided in any one of the girls, they would have told me to go to a doctor and find out. But I didn't know you could do that.

My plan was to leave the company in some big city, and find a house for unwed mothers. I'd leave a note for the stage manager, so nobody would try to trace me. My leaving wouldn't matter to the show. My understudy would be very happy.

I knew about homes where you could go to have your baby and give it up for adoption, because Papa had made a movie about this. The movie showed how the young woman didn't have to give the name of the father or of her parents. She could just have the baby and leave. I figured no one would ever know. I'd write to my family and say the tour had been extended.

My big problem was that I was sending Papa half of my weekly paycheck, but I'd think of something.

But I didn't need to do any of this. We'd been on the road for about three weeks, and I had a normal period.

A Woman Scorned

During the nine-month tour, my skin healed. I was thinking how nice it would be to return and show the man who had healed me.

And maybe we would get to know each other.

I told my friend Joyce what I was thinking. Joyce got very upset. She knew him. She said they had been lovers. He had promised to marry her. She said he'd ruined her life. She wept as she told me. I felt very angry at him for what he had done to her.

When I got back to Hollywood, I did go to see him. But only to tell him what I thought of him.

I boasted that I planned to have many lovers in my life, but that he wouldn't be one of them. I felt I was getting vengeance for my friend Joyce. Also scorning him before he scorned me.

I remember being surprised at the look on his face. But I left before he could speak.

A couple of years later, I found out Joyce was famous for her stories about all the different men in Hollywood who had ruined her. She wasn't telling me the truth.

But I never tried to see the man again. Maybe I was embarrassed at what I'd said the last time I saw him.

Could he have been a man I could have really loved? Probably not.

But I'll never know.

Maybe he just cared for crippled people. And knew I was one of them.

ONCE PAPA TOLD ME about a guide who was taking him over a glacier in New Zealand. They came to a deep crevasse. The guide jumped over to the other side. Papa looked down and froze.

The guide had Papa stretch out his hand. The guide touched his fingers to Papa's fingers. That was all it took for Papa to get to the other side.

But I didn't believe I needed a guide. I didn't even know I was wandering lost on an ice mountain.

All by myself.

PART 8

Not Wanted

27

Always to Be

MY WINDOW THIS morning. The warmth of my room has cleared the glass. The first light of dawn is outlining the trees, etching delicate beauty where before I saw nothing but darkness.

> *Hope springs eternal*
> *In the human breast.*
> *Man never is*
> *But always to be blessed.*

In the Advanced English Literature class at Hollywood High School our teacher enjoyed telling us that Alexander Pope was right. We live, we die, and there is no blessing for us ever.

But what if the blessing is in the hope itself? The hope we have burning in us, here, now, and forever in the eternal.

I hope when I finish this book it will be a butterfly that goes in fluttering flight out my window, out of my sight, dancing in the sunlit air, around the corner of Main Street and Stanard.

What if its bright colors briefly catch the eye of a few people on their way?

I would like that.

But I hope I don't lose sight of the new-every-morning view out my window, nor of the burning in me for the day's work that is to be.

Playing a Role for Papa

Antique furniture! I came home from the nine-month *Song of Norway* tour to find our house crammed full of somebody else's antique furniture. Stuffed into every room of our house. Always our houses had been such private places where each one of us lived in our own little world. But now Papa had brought a producer, Renson, into our midst. We were hiding his furniture so his wife wouldn't know about it until after their divorce.

Papa and Renson were making a half-hour movie, a TV pilot, that Renson was sure he could sell.

They asked me to go with them to the Superstition Mountains in Arizona. Renson, Papa, and I squeezed together in the front seat of the Lincoln convertible with camera equipment piled up in the backseat and in the trunk.

It was the only time I ever worked with Papa.

I was a double for an old man! I wore a beard and wig and dusty baggy pants. And an old floppy hat which I'd fallen in love with. It was soft felt. I was hoping I'd get to keep it.

Papa was so far away from me with his camera, you couldn't know I was a woman. I had to struggle backwards up a steep narrow trail, yanking and pulling at a rope around a mule's neck. It was so hot and dry I could see flies crawling up the mule's nose and sipping moisture from its eyes.

At one point, the mule jerks its head! Its hoofs slip and send loose rocks over the edge of the trail. Rocks tumbling down the side of the steep mountain to the dry canyon below. I'm afraid I'll be next. Papa yells: "Bang! Bang!"

A gunshot! My cue! I fall dead on the trail. It's lucky I have the man's wig, because my floppy hat comes off when I fall. Renson steps out of his hiding place. He is the villain. He kicks my hat over the edge of the cliff. He stands over my body. Papa is very pleased with the whole scene.

Later, Renson told me that during that trip he knew he was in love with me.

Not Wanted

The TV people said the film was wonderful. But not right for them. Renson finally sold it to an art film distributor. He said the money didn't cover the cost. Mama asked Papa how much it sold for. Papa didn't know. Renson handled all the money in their little company.

About six months after my trip with Papa and Renson to the Superstition Mountains, Renson asked me to marry him. By then I believed I was in love with him. I said yes. We planned to marry as soon as his divorce was final.

The Red-Headed Man

"We knew you were safe with Renson," Mama said. "Because he was homosexual. Your father and I both knew this."

I was sitting in the visiting room of the nursing home with Mama, about a year before she died. I said, "Mama! You knew this? And you were going to let me marry him?"

I don't remember how she responded. So many times I can remember my questions to my parents, but not the answers they gave me.

That day in the nursing home, Mama talked about the red-headed man who had come pounding on our front door, angrily shouting at Papa and Mama. He wanted Renson. Papa and Mama said Renson wasn't there. But the man pushed his way into our house.

I remember how shocked I was to see him shove my parents aside and go running through our house. Our home! He ran from room to room, screaming for Renson.

Renson went running out the back door.
The red-headed man followed him into our backyard.
Renson ran into the neighbor's backyard.
The red-headed man gave up.

I can still see him standing, watching Renson disappear. Then sitting down in the dirt and ashes by our incinerator. Crying and sobbing about love and betrayal. I thought Renson had stolen his girlfriend.

THE MAN NEVER came back. None of us ever mentioned him until the day Mama talked about him to me in the nursing home.

Pantaloon, 1.

28

What Does a Cat Know?

I OPEN MY WINDOW to snow.

> **snow,** The aqueous vapor of the atmo-
> sphere precipitated in a crystalline
> form, and falling to the earth in flakes
> characterized by their whiteness and
> lightness.

Crystalline wafers floating past my window, falling back and forth and down, down to the alley below. Frozen aqueous vapor that started secretly sneaking down during the night while I slept.

> *And when the dew fell upon the camp*
> *in the night, the manna fell upon it.*
> Numbers 11:9

I hear a sound in the alley. Rhythmic thump-crunch of footsteps in the snow. I go close to the glass to look down. A man walking, bundled up. In Prague the padded quilted jacket he's wearing is called a Bundy. He's all bundled up in his Bundy. It looks like he's just walking for the fun of it. But why in the alley? Why not see this white purity floating down in the beauty of the city park? Or at least on historic old Main Street.

The man in the Bundy is gone. No sound now. Once more just the secret silent magic flakes of snow, white wafers, Eucharist manna, softly falling to and fro in the gentle wind.

I know the snow is beautiful. So why do I feel like complaining? Why do I want it to be my usual window? Just showing me one little thing each morning. This snow piling up is like all that I've written. It's too much. My book has me snowed in, snowbound.

> **snowed,** Submerged, overpowered,
> ***deceived*** by overwhelming details.

Deceived? No! Deception is the Dwarf Woman's domain. Not mine.

The Dwarf Woman didn't get me when I was three years old, she's not going to get me now.

I have stories to write.

Stories that keep coming to me.

Gifts I keep unwrapping every day.

Stories about my father.

My mother.

My sister.

My brother.

Stories about my cat.

Green Olive

The room is dark. The only source of light is a standing gooseneck lamp shining down over the shoulder of a man sitting at a large desk.

The desk is a costly antique with inlaid wood so precisely formed that the fleur-de-lis pattern looks to have grown miraculously within the trunk of a single tree.

The room is jammed full of a discordant mixture of costly antiques and cheap furniture.

A coffee table from the Goodwill.

A Tiffany lamp with an empty socket, no light shines through the myriad pieces of colored glass in the shade.

A love seat with furniture crammed against it, so no one can sit on the tight satin brocade and velvet cushions.

A sleek grey cat is on the love seat.

The man at the desk turns the pages of his movie script.

The cat digs her paws delicately into the soft velvet cushions.

The man adds a note to the many notes written in the margin.

The cat snuggles into the nest she's made for herself.

She's a small cat. Her name is Green Olive. A creature of power and grace but with a strange scarred face.

The man is unaware of the cat on the love seat, doesn't know she has claimed this forbidden territory as her own.

Outside the window, the moon shines down on the old wood-frame house on the hill, and makes mysterious, shadow shapes of the shirts and pants hanging on the clothesline. The moon changes the backyard incinerator into a freestanding sculpture.

Inside the house, an old grandfather clock chimes once.

The man, Elmer Clifton, stands, stretches, looks down at the script on the desk, turns off the light, and leaves the room.

The cat, Green Olive, rises up, arches her back, sinks her claws again and again into the tight satin brocade of the antique love seat.

The moon sends a silver stream through the window.

Little Enough to Sacrifice

The day Green Olive showed up at our back screen door, her bones pro-truded all along the ridge of her spine. When she let us pet her, she felt like a skeleton with fur stretched over it.

Mama made fun of her. Said she had an ugly face because of the scar over one eye. I thought the scar gave her a look of mystery.

She ate whatever we gave her. Mama and I just scraped food off the plates into her dish. She lost her spiny look and became sleek and swift and beautifully coordinated, but still people said her face looked odd with the scar.

One night when Mama and I were doing the dishes, I went to empty scraps onto her dish. It wasn't in its usual place.

Mama started running the rinse water hard and fast. She said, "I had to take Green Olive to the pound."

"Why?" I felt like my ears were filling with the rushing water.

Mama didn't look at me. "I had to get rid of her. She wouldn't stop scratching the upholstery on Renson's love seat."

I had an odd sensation that I could hear Green Olive crying outside in the dark. I almost went to look. I picked up a towel and started wiping a plate around and around.

I said, "She never did that to our furniture."

Mama said, "I don't think she likes Renson."

Mama left the kitchen to go wipe off the dining room table. "Don't worry, by now somebody has given her a home."

"Mama! Nobody would take Green Olive out of the pound! Not with beautiful cats all around her."

From the dining room Mama's voice came to me small and tight. "You can't know that."

My response came out loud and harsh. "You sneaked her out of the house! Papa would never have let you do it!"

"He doesn't even know she's gone!" Mama came back to the sink, moving as fast as she could to get the dishes done. "Your father has more important things on his mind than an alley cat. And don't you tell him! He'll be afraid Renson will notice the shredded upholstery. I tried to sew it up, but it still shows."

I was still wiping round and round on the same plate.

She grabbed the towel from me. "I liked her, too, but she had to go!" She dried her hands. "It's little enough for us to sacrifice." She threw down the towel. "Do you realize Renson is talking to Ida Lupino and Collier Young? And they just might finance The MOVIE?"

The MOVIE. It was a magic word in our house. It would give Papa back his rightful position in Hollywood. Once more he'd be the great director that he was in the silent movie days.

I followed Mama out of the kitchen. "I wish Renson could sell his antiques."

"You know he wants to, but he can't! Not until his divorce is final. His wife would take the money."

Mama went into the bathroom and closed the door. That was the way she and I often ended conversations with each other.

I finished the dishes without her.

We never mentioned Green Olive again.

29

Crate in the Water

Two Dreams in the Night

FIRST DREAM

I see my hand aiming a squirt gun at the Brownsville Fire Department sign. As the gun squirts water, the big door rises up and the fire engine comes roaring out of the station on its way to save a burning house.

SECOND DREAM

A boat. Alone in the middle of the empty ocean. It's a moonlit night.

I am in the boat. Safe. Up away from, out of, the dark water. The boat is pulling in its wake a large crate with precious cargo sealed inside.

I choose to get out of the boat, into the water. To be closer to the crate.

But once in the water, I look around in fear. The boat is gone. It's only me, alone in the water with the crate. The crate is floating, but submerged about a foot beneath the surface of the water.

Being under water, it will be heavy, heavy, but I know I must pull it alone. To shore. To a shore I cannot see. It will be heavy, heavy, but dream knowledge tells me that I can do it; others are with me.

THE CRATE IS my writing.

Heavier, now that it is under the surface.

From now on, I must be with it in the water.

WHEN I LISTEN to Michael's tape, his story doesn't seem heavy to him. My story, especially the part of the book coming up, is heavy for me.

Michael speaks of early confusion in his life. In my life, it was early and late confusion. I kept struggling with Mama's conflicting messages. Part of their power over me was because Mama believed what she was saying.

For instance, she really believed she had married Papa before Pat was conceived.

Once, when I was about twelve years old, I heard her talking angrily on the phone. She was upset about somebody's cousin who had left her parents' home to have her own apartment. "Any woman who does that sort of thing is after one thing, and one thing only! A man! She's got hot pants for a man!"

She made it sound so awful—having hot pants for a man. I promised myself I never would.

ONCE MAMA CALLED me a prostitute.

> **prostitute, 1.** To offer to a lewd use, to
> surrender one's body for base purposes.

I was standing in the living room holding an empty cup. From the kitchen, Mama was yelling prostitute, prostitute!

I stood perfectly still. A power that wasn't me seemed to come up through the floorboards, through the soles of my feet, rising up and ending in my hands.

I looked down. I was looking down at a broken cup in my hands. I'd broken it without knowing it.

There was blood. I'd cut myself. It frightened me.

My voice came out in a squeezed whisper. "Mama. Look what I've done to myself."

If the Shoe Fits, Wear It

Maybe I believed Mama was speaking the truth. Maybe I was prostituting myself. Ever since the trip to the Superstition Mountains, Renson had been making love to me.

> **prostitute, 2.** Given over, devoted,
> exposed, subjected to any destructive
> agency. To prostitute one's talents.

A month after calling me a prostitute, Mama handed me a *Reader's Digest* with a how-to-do-it article about keeping your chastity intact until after your marriage. "Read this," Mama said. "Forewarned is forearmed."

I reminded her that she'd called me a prostitute. I could see she was completely thrown by this. She denied it. Said I was making it up. She really believed she could never have called her own daughter such a thing.

But she did. I still remember.

Engaged to Be Married

Once, Papa and I and Renson had gone to a nightclub with some people who were thinking of investing money in their company. A young man came to our table. He was from South America. He asked Renson's permission to dance with me. He thought Renson, the man I was engaged to marry, was my father. I was afraid Renson's feelings had been hurt, but he just laughed and told me to dance with the young man.

I was nervous on the dance floor. I carefully explained how I was a trained dancer, but didn't know how to ballroom dance.

The young man assured me that I was doing fine. "I could teach you the dances of my country," he said. "Would you like that?"

I said yes. The next day Mama heard me on the phone arranging to rent a rehearsal room for the young man and myself at Perry's Rehearsal Studio.

Perry's was a joke with dancers. It was such a decrepit place! Run by old vaudeville people who had their glossy photographs and theater posters all over the walls.

For fifty cents, you could rent a big empty room with mirrors covering one wall. And a phonograph player, but you had to bring your own phonograph needle.

When I hung up, Mama was standing right behind me. "Just what do you think you're doing, young lady?"

I told her about the young man from South America. How he was proud of his country's dances and wanted to teach them to me.

Mama made me call Perry's back and cancel the room. "You're engaged to be married," she said. "You don't go out with other men!"

I was happy to hear her say I was engaged. Up until that moment I'd known Papa was all for my marriage to Renson, but I hadn't known how Mama felt about it.

It Was a Sunday

I'd just come from signing the papers to buy a house! Renson had fallen in love with it! So we bought it! It was the kind of spontaneous, wonderful, crazy thing people in love do. Because of his divorce, still not final, he couldn't sign the papers. But I could!

When Renson dropped me off at home, I came bursting into the house, so sure Papa and Mama would be so happy with my news.

I can still see the three of us. Papa standing like a statue. Me burning with joy and at the same time wondering why Papa had that terrible look of fear frozen on his face. He looked like he couldn't move.

Mama's fear was exploding all over the room. "You fool! What have you done?"

I started screaming like Mama, "It's my life! I'm twenty-one years old!"

Mama was coming at me like she would strangle me. "Who is to pay?"

"Renson! He just couldn't sign the papers! Because his divorce isn't final!"

Papa never said one word. Never moved. His eyes looking right through me. I don't know how long he stood there. I ran out of the house.

The next day, Ida Lupino decided to put up the money for Papa's movie, *Not Wanted*. Everything else was forgotten.

Pressure

A few months after Papa died, I heard Mama on the phone telling a story about how Papa had come home one day and told her that he'd been standing on the corner of Gower and Hollywood Boulevard, waiting for Renson to pick him up in the car, when suddenly he realized that his briefcase had landed on the sidewalk at his feet. He hadn't felt himself dropping it. He wanted to stoop and pick it up. But he couldn't! For a few moments, he couldn't move. And then, he could.

Mama said, "The doctors decided it was his teeth, poisoning his system. So he was going to the dentist to get his teeth fixed. But it wasn't his teeth! It was all the pressure he was under."

When Mama said pressure, I thought of the pressure I'd put him under that Sunday when I came home with the news that I'd bought a house with Renson.

PRESSURE. I CAN'T remember what ever happened to those papers I signed to buy that house. I can't remember. Can't remember anyone ever talking about that house. The memory is all gone. Evanescent. But that strange fearful look on Papa's face. His eyes staring right through me.

That scene. That Sunday. That I cannot forget.

AT HIS FUNERAL Mama said, "Your father would not have wanted to live a cripple."

30

Maiden in a Myth

THE YOUNG WOMAN stands on the trapeze, gripping the slippery sidebars, suspended high in the air. She wears a one-piece Esther Williams swimsuit. Under her bare feet, the iron bar is cold and hard.

She braces herself, bends her knees as the machinery pulls her trapeze back and up. The noise of grinding gears reverberates in the hollow expanse of the huge soundstage. She ends in a crouch, holding tight to the iron sidebars as she reaches the top of the arc.

Her body faces down. Directly beneath her metal funnels belch up clouds of colored smoke.

Her trapeze stops with a jerk.

Her bare foot slips off the crossbar.

She looks down with fear. What if she fell? Could she somehow throw herself beyond those sharp metal chimneys? Dive safely into the water? Or would she end up impaled on the smoking metal funnels?

The other divers sit huddled together at the edge of the pool. They stare at the smoke rising up to the young woman on her trapeze. They see the smoke curl around their own trapezes, hanging empty, each above its own cluster of smoking funnels.

One of the men jumps up, angry. "The smoke we knew about! But who said anything about those chimneys right below us."

"It's probably in our contracts."

A thin woman knits rapidly as she speaks in a high, shrill voice, "It's the heat I'm afraid of. Just think what it'll be when we start shooting! All those arc lights burning up there! No way for that hot air to escape!"

A soundstage has no windows. The walls and ceiling are covered with thick, grey, quilted soundproofing.

The thin woman points her knitting needle up at the catwalks. "How many electricians have fallen off those catwalks? Fainting with the trapped heat!"

The high narrow catwalks hang suspended, close to the ceiling, like jungle bridges crisscrossing over a deep canyon.

"And we're as high as those catwalks!"

"We could be killed!"

"Did anybody read the fine print?"

"Why are we doing this?"

"Money."

The thin woman points at the cloud that now conceals the young woman on her trapeze. "She's doing it for love! Her whole paycheck goes to her father!"

"I'm doing it for love!" Elgin says. "Love of money!"

Elgin is always trying to make them laugh. "Look at the bright side! This is India! Those smoke pots are our burial pyres. If we land on them, the studio saves on funeral expenses."

The thin woman gasps. "Don't say that! It'll make it happen!"

"No, it won't," Elgin says. "The gods will hear us laughing! And they'll let us live! For our entertainment value!"

By the third day of rehearsals, the divers are all making jokes about their fears. There's not much laughter, but everyone believes the joking brings them good luck.

And then comes the first day of shooting.

The twelve divers stand in a line on their twelve trapezes. The grinding machines lift them high in the air. Nauseous smoke rises up. They can't see each other. They can't see the water below them. They're all alone in the cloud.

Below, the choreographer and the cinematographer watch and wait for the exact moment when the dense cloud billows up in just the right spectacular Technicolor fantasy shape for the magical flying creatures to come soaring through.

In this foul-smelling cloud, the divers on their trapezes crouch like crabs waiting to be sprung, the blanket of chemical fog pressing against their eyeballs, while the camera crew debates.

Focus for Balance

The young woman's trapeze is the third from the end. She waits with her body suspended above the chimneys far below. She holds her head up, her eyes focused on a small white sign she's discovered directly across the soundstage on the opposite wall, too far away to read. Even when the smoke blocks her view, she maintains her vigil, imagines her eyes are still connecting in with that one white spot in space.

Suddenly. No warning. Just that wrenching jerk, and she is swinging down to the bottom of the arc, then up the other side to the top, where her feet push off the iron bar, and she is diving through the dense smoke into clear air.

The scream comes while she is in midair. It pulses with the pressure of the air she is diving through. She hits the surface of the water, it rushes by her ears. The height of the dive forces her down to the cement bottom of the pool. Too fast. The scream has made her forget that she must turn and head for the surface. Just before she reaches the cement, she arches up. She is safe. She has completed the dive.

But what was that scream?

Elgin.

His trapeze had twisted and flung him off. The crossbar hit his head and knocked him out.

His body misses the platform of smoking funnels, hits the water, and sinks.

As the other divers swim to the surface, Elgin's blood rises up with them, dyeing the water red, then dissolving into pale pink ripples around them as they tread water.

Elgin almost drowns before the lifeguards get to him. They carry him out of the soundstage on a stretcher.

All the male dancers quit. Even though the studio reports that Elgin wasn't badly hurt, the men won't get back on the trapezes. They say the money isn't worth it.

All the women stay on the job.

The young woman doesn't even think of quitting. She is a character in a myth. She is in love. Her love gives her courage. She is performing an act of valor. To prove herself worthy of the love of the king, her father. And of his prince, Renson.

The young woman doesn't tell her father or Renson about Elgin's accident. She believes if they knew what could happen to her, they wouldn't let her keep doing it.

Busby Berkeley's Gun

The trapeze sequence for this MGM Esther Williams spectacular was directed by the New York choreographer Busby Berkeley. In dance history books you can read how Busby Berkeley used to shoot off a gun to cue the dancers during rehearsals of his *Ziegfeld Follies* musicals on Broadway.

When I worked for him in Hollywood, he was an old man, but he still had his gun. He shot it off to get all of us dancers to dive off our trapezes at the same moment. Actually it wasn't safe to leave the trapeze until it had swung to the top of the arc.

We all ignored Busby Berkeley's gun. He didn't know this because he couldn't see us at the moment we left our trapezes. We were hidden inside the thick cloud of colored smoke.

Busby Berkeley kept demanding that we come through the cloud in a straight line. It was simple, he screamed. All we had to do was leave our trapezes when he shot off his gun.

He thought I was the only one who didn't obey his gun, because the others all came through the cloud together. They were together because they all weighed about the same. I was only a hundred and ten pounds, so my trapeze didn't reach the top of the arc with the others.

By the time I came soaring through the cloud, the others already had their heads down aiming for the water. I'd finish my solo flight and hit the water, knowing that Busby Berkeley would be waiting for me when I came to the surface. He'd be storming at the side of the pool. Waving his smoking gun and swearing at me.

I'd have lost my job, except the man in charge of the trapeze mechanism figured out how to stagger our starting points so my dive matched the others.

In the chorus of Singing in the Rain, *1952*

Evanescent Stardom Fading, Fading, Fading

I had all the work I could do, as long as I was willing to be in the chorus. My agent said being a chorus girl was ruining my chances of becoming a star. But now that Renson had come into our lives, Papa didn't need me to be a star. He just needed me to make money until Renson and he got The MOVIE made.

My agent didn't want me doing chorus work. He said I was throwing away my career. He kept calling me to go on interviews for speaking parts.

But I could never go because I was working as a chorus girl.

Finally my agent gave up on me.

ON TOP OF WORLD! Hand on hip, Doris Day struts gaily, as chorus girl in "April in Paris," at Warners' Hollywood, Downtown and Wiltern. She's just been picked to be Miss America

Dirinda Reads How Girls Get Rich

Dirinda Clifton, one of Nick Castle's beauties for the chorus line of Paramount's "Here Come the Girls," spends her spare time bolstering cherished traditions in this changing world.

Dirinda's idea involves relaxing between scenes of the Technicolor musical with a good book.

31

A Persistent Error

NOT MUCH SLEEP last night. Up before dawn. I'm at my computer. Too early for daylight.

Window Painted Black

My mood matches my window. There used to be a song: "Color Me Black." It was a take-off on the instructions in a child's coloring book telling what color to make each part of the picture.

Through my black window, I see one small light. Shining through the trees. I've never noticed that one light before.

I have Papa's photo albums piled up on the floor. All of them have black covers except the small one with Polly Anna in it.

The light in the window just went out. I keep looking at the dark.

The photographs in the albums are all black and white. No color in those days. The albums are all that's left of the world trip and the thousands of feet of film Papa shot. All that film! And not one movie that he wanted to make came out of it.

Then, in the last days of his life, he was making The MOVIE. It was called *Not Wanted*. Ida Lupino had put up the money. Finally he was making a movie he wanted to make. But on the third day of shooting, he had a cerebral thrombosis right in the middle of directing a scene.

Not Wanted
This picture was taken in 1949.
    The year Papa died.
    I study his face.
    My eyes tell me I'm looking at a man
    who would have chosen to live.

But, that's not what Mama believed.

> **delusion, 1.** A false impression or be-
> lief, a misleading of the mind.

Mama said, "Your father would not have wanted to live a cripple." I know this is what she believed. But I don't know what made her believe this.

> **delusion, 2.** A persistent error of a
> deranged mind.

> *It had all been a voluntary, self-created*
> *delusion.*
>
> Jane Austen

In the Hospital Room

On the bed his right hand moved.

Just enough to write notes.

He couldn't move his head to see what he was writing. He had me move the pieces of paper so that he could put down each letter one after the other. I didn't tell him that nobody could read his notes.

The doctors and nurses talked with Mama in the hall. I didn't know she was telling them not to operate.

> **delusion, 3.** A perception which fails
> to give the true character of an object
> perceived.

Mama said, "Your father would not have wanted to live a cripple."

Head of Greek Statue,
6th cent. B.C., show-
ing Archaic Smile.

32

Point of View

MY HUNDRED-YEAR-OLD window. Having only one window makes me concentrate on the life I can see within its perimeter.

> **perimeter,** The continuous line forming the boundary of a closed geometrical figure.

My view is tempered by defects in the antique glass. If I hold very still, the outside appears one way. If I slightly lift or lower my head, the images I see waver like reflections on ripples of water.

The hundred-year-old glass is my Walden Pond.

Was the glass made with these trembling waves, or did they come with old age? Or is it my eyes? Deceiving me?

> **optics,** An instrument for investigating the *discriminative* powers of the retina.

Mama's Discriminative Powers

Papa lies on the hospital bed.

Flat on his back.

He cannot talk.

Most of him cannot move at all.

But he can hear.

And he can signal with his right hand.

Mama uses her discriminative powers to reach the conclusion that Papa would not want to live as a cripple.

> **discriminate, 1.** To distinguish with
> the mind, to perceive nice differences.

At the funeral, Mama told me that the doctors had asked her to let them operate. They said they could save his life, but he would be a cripple.

> **discriminate, 2.** To distinguish accu-
> rately; as, to discriminate between fact
> and fancy.

Mama said, "Your father would not have wanted to live a cripple."

> *To make an anxious discrimination*
> *between the miracle absolute and*
> *providential.*
>
> Trench

AUNT GRACE SAID all Papa's family lived a long time.

This is a picture of Papa's great-uncle George who lived to be ninety. He was Uncle Hilton's father.

This is a picture of Uncle Hilton. Before he was a cripple. The caption in the photo album doesn't say why he's all dressed up, so jaunty, so debonair, standing on the wet sand with his shoes brightly polished.

Maybe it's a joke.

Papa said Hilton loved to kid around.

The next picture is Hilton with his arms around his two army buddies. The caption "Singing Trio" is a joke. You turn the picture over and it says, "We never sing."

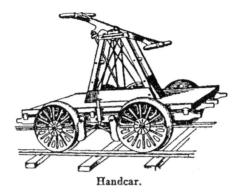

Handcar.

Late one night, celebrating the end of World War I, Hilton and his two friends were on their way home from a party.

All three were very drunk.

They decided to take a ride on a small, flat, hand-driven railway car.

Hilton was singing to the rhythm of his two friends pumping the handle up and down.

They got the handcar going very fast.

Hilton fell off on the railway tracks. The iron wheels ran over him. He lived another fifty years. His back wouldn't bend. He couldn't walk.

Uncle Hilton and Aunt Grace were the only people I remember our family visiting. We went to their house on our Sunday drives.

They let me go into their bedroom and get the pastel crayons and paper they kept for me on the bottom shelf of their closet.

Their bed was higher than normal beds. It had a swinging bar over it. In the mornings Hilton must have hoisted himself up, to swing himself over, and get onto the rolling, slanting bed that Aunt Grace wheeled into the living room every day.

I liked visiting their home. I would draw pictures with their pastels, and listen to Uncle Hilton and Papa talking and laughing. Papa used to say that being a cripple hadn't made Hilton lose his sense of humor.

MAMA SAID, "Your father would not have wanted to live a cripple."

How did she know?
Did she ask him?
He could signal yes or no.
Did she ask him?

The hospital where Papa died was an old brown brick building in the middle of downtown Los Angeles.

Papa's room had only one bed. One window that looked out on an air shaft with a brown brick wall. If I forced open the window, and stuck my head out, I could see a square of sky five stories above. A square of cement four stories below.

I remember the hours and hours of sitting by his bed. Only his breathing going in and out.

He could hear.

People shouted at him.

They thought they had to shout. But I talked to him in a regular voice, and he heard me.

33

The Show Must Go On

PAPA WAS IN the middle of directing The MOVIE, *Not Wanted*, when a blood vessel exploded in his brain. I was working in *Annie Get Your Gun* at MGM. I was just a showgirl, so they let me off to be with Papa in the hospital.

Papa couldn't talk. Most of the day it was just he and I alone in the hospital room.

Papa didn't know that he was through as the director of the movie. I didn't know this either until I phoned Renson from the hospital lobby the first evening. I said, "Renson, he's going to be all right. The doctors say—"

Renson interrupted me, shouting, "I have good news, too! We kept right on shooting!"

At first I didn't understand. How could they keep shooting with no director? Then I heard Renson saying that Ida Lupino had taken over the directing.

"She's a great little trouper! It's going to be just what your father wanted."

I wondered why Renson was shouting. Or maybe he wasn't. Maybe it was just that I'd been sitting so many hours, in the silent room, with Papa. Maybe that's why I had trouble talking to him.

"Renson. It's Papa's movie. He's the director. You have to wait for him."

"My dear, it would cost thousands of dollars if we closed down production. The show must go on. If anyone understands this great rule of show business, it's your father."

I heard Renson's voice going on and on as I was hanging up.

I didn't tell Papa they weren't waiting for him. Nobody else told him. Not many people in Hollywood even knew he was in the hospital. Renson explained to Mama that it wouldn't be good publicity for the movie. People in show business are very superstitious, he said. They might take it as a bad omen if it were known that Papa had been struck down right in the middle of the shooting.

In the Hospital Room

Papa lay with his eyes on the ceiling while his right hand moved just enough to write notes. He thought he was communicating with Renson about The MOVIE. I couldn't tell him that his notes were going nowhere.

I'd pick them up and hold them so he could see me going through the door with them. I'd stay away long enough so that he would believe the note had reached the office at the studio. I must have been just as out of touch with reality as he was.

At the moment Papa died, he was writing a note to Renson. I was the only one with him. I had my eyes centered in on his fingers as if my concentration would help him keep writing.

That's when I heard the sound. I had never heard it before, but I knew right away what it was. I'd always thought the death rattle was something writers of melodramas dreamed up. But I heard Papa's death rattle. I heard the life come clattering up out of his body while he was still laboring to get the next word down on the paper.

The Funeral Package

Before the funeral service began, Mama and I were standing by the open casket. Mama was rubbing her fingers on the wood of the casket.

She said, "Your father would never have wanted to live a cripple."

Mama was leaning over the casket, adjusting the scarf around Papa's neck. "I told the doctors not to operate."

Mama straightened up, still looking at Papa lying in the casket. Waiting for me to say something to her.

I kept my eyes on Papa lying in the casket. He had on his favorite silk scarf around his neck, and the burgundy pants from the London Shop. The London Shop was an expensive, exclusive men's haberdashery next to the Roosevelt Hotel on Hollywood Boulevard. We saved up money so Papa could go there. Clothes were an important part of the image he presented to Hollywood. Sometimes there'd be no meat on the table for awhile. We'd eat macaroni and cheese. Boston baked beans. Split pea soup with corn bread. Spanish rice. Food I still love.

The organ was playing a trite song Papa would have hated. I had thought of playing the first part of the *Moonlight Sonata*.

Papa liked me playing the *Moonlight Sonata*. He told me once he'd been caught in a snowstorm and sought refuge in a big, falling-down mansion. An old man let him in, and while Papa waited out the storm, the old man played the whole Beethoven sonata on his concert grand piano.

Papa said that when the old man got to the third part, the movement called *The Storm*, the trees outside the tall French doors went wild, raging with wind and blizzard snow.

After Papa told me this story I tried very hard to play the second and third movements for him, but they were too hard for me.

Papa's funeral was a package deal which couldn't include me playing the *Moonlight Sonata*.

Not Wanted

A few days after the funeral, when Mama went back to the office at the studio, expecting to do her secretary job, she found that Renson had cleared out all her things. He'd packed them into a cardboard box and set the box outside the door.

Papa's things, too. His coffee mug. And his magnifying glass in its leather case. The silver pen that he saved for signing important papers.

Everything was in the one cardboard box outside the locked door. Including Mama's teacup. And the makeup that she'd kept at the office.

Mama had given up wearing makeup, but when Renson came along, he'd talked her into using it again. And getting a new haircut. She found clothes at the Salvation Army Store that she redesigned and made beautiful.

Renson gave her a new image of herself—the sophisticated secretary. She believed it!

But the day she brought home that cardboard box, her image was all shrunk down and buried inside it. There was a note that said a friend of Ida Lupino would now be the secretary in Mama's place.

I have tears in my eyes writing this. I remember the ashen look of Mama that day. She hadn't known Papa's death would be the end of her job. I remember how I felt seeing Mama coming into the house carrying that cardboard box.

It could be that the day my mother came home with that cardboard box in her arms was the day her spirit for life started to die.

A Silver Lining

I didn't cry when Papa died. I thought I would later. But I didn't.

I went back to being a showgirl on the *Annie Get Your Gun* movie. I had only been away a week. That job lasted six months, which was good, because Mama, Michael, and I needed the money.

We were shooting outside on the back lot of Metro-Goldwyn-Mayer. It was the big climax scene where Annie Oakley is up on the grandstand shooting her gun and singing her big love song to Buffalo Bill.

We showgirls were lined up behind her in our cowgirl outfits. I felt exposed, like all the extras and workers were looking at me standing up there on that grandstand.

During breaks, people I didn't know would come to me and tell me how sorry they were for me.

"I know just how you're feeling," they'd say.

The trouble is I didn't feel anything. I thought there was something very wrong with me because I didn't feel what they told me I was feeling.

Once I caught myself laughing at a joke the director had made over the loudspeaker. Everybody saw me standing up on that grandstand laughing when Papa had just died!

From then on I made myself look sad except when the camera was rolling. I guess I succeeded because one of the extras, an old vaudeville character I recognized from Perry's Rehearsal Studio, came up to me one day. She patted me on the shoulder. "I can see you're hurting, Honey," she said, "but you're a real trouper. You go on with the show!"

Then she started singing how every cloud has a silver lining.

It

A couple of months after Papa's death, I thought I might be pregnant. I never told Mama. She didn't know Renson had been making love to me. I went to the medical clinic. They said they'd phone me the results of the test. Mama wasn't home at the time the call came, so she never knew anything about it. The test proved that I was pregnant.

I didn't think of it as a baby. It was an it. A month went by. Then it naturally aborted. That's what the doctor said.

The morning it happened, I thought I had a stomachache. I didn't know I was losing a baby. I went to the bathroom and sat on the toilet. And out it came. This thing like a three-inch bloody mummy splashing into the toilet bowl. I needed to throw up, but I made myself fish it out of the water first.

I wrapped it up in tissues, but the blood seeped through. So I covered it with aluminum wrap, and took it to the clinic. The nurse looked distastefully at it. But how was I to know I didn't have to bring it to the doctor?

I wondered why it had died. But I didn't ask the doctor. I'd never met him before. Each time I came to the clinic it was a different doctor who examined me.

I asked the nurse if it was a boy or a girl. She must have thought I was making a poor joke. She just looked at me as if I were to blame for the death. Maybe I was. I never wanted it.

Bambino of Andrea della Robbia.

The Two Movers

Mama said once that Renson went to prison. I read somewhere he was at Columbia Pictures. I never saw him again.

He lied about his divorce not being final. I found this out when two moving men were carrying his antiques out of our house. I was hidden at the top of the stairs. They didn't know I was listening to them.

FIRST MOVER
So where we taking this stuff?

SECOND MOVER
To his ex-wife. She was supposed to have it
two years ago when their divorce was final.

FIRST MOVER
How do you know all this?

SECOND MOVER
My wife reads all the Hollywood gossip.
The guy's name is Renson. He's being sued.

FIRST MOVER
By the divorced wife?

SECOND MOVER
No, by people who gave him money for a movie.
They say he kept most of it for himself.
But he says the old director, his partner, stole it.

FIRST MOVER
Did he?

SECOND MOVER
Who knows? He's dead.

FIRST MOVER
What was the director's name?

SECOND MOVER
I don't remember.

I looked out the window and saw the two men at their truck loading Renson's love seat. I saw where Green Olive had dug her claws into the satin brocade.

Is That You, Green Olive?

I didn't tell Mama, but when the moving men were gone, I went to the animal pound.

I walked up and down the rows of cages. The cats seemed content in their cages. Some were purring. Green Olive wouldn't have been purring. She'd have been clawing at the wire to get out!

I came upon a grey cat with dark streaks. She was asleep, curled up, all I could see was her back. I whispered. "Is that you, Green Olive?"

She looked up. A pretty face.

I left the room of cages.

In the reception room the woman behind the counter said, "No luck?" At first, I didn't realize she was talking to me. I felt I was there and not there at the same time.

I said, "It's been a long time. I knew she wouldn't be here. But I had to prove it to myself."

"So somebody took her home."

"No. She had an ugly face. Nobody would have wanted her."

"You have to give yourself another one."

I smiled. Didn't answer. I knew I'd never want another.

Is That You, Green Olive?

I knew Green Olive was dead, yet I kept expecting her to come home. Even years later, I'd see a cat that looked even a little bit like her, and I'd find myself saying, "Is that you, Green Olive?" I even thought I saw her one night in St. Louis! I was touring with an Edwin Lester musical.

It was after the show. A bunch of us dancers were going into a German place down by the river. It was famous for its potato pancakes. My friends had gone on through the door, but I'd stopped to watch a boat going by on the river, lights dim, a silhouette slipping by in the fog.

Just as I was about to turn away I noticed a cat that looked like Green Olive. She was down by the jetty, crouched, ready to spring. Before I could stop myself, I whispered: "Is that you, Green Olive?"

A Dream in the Night

I hold a little black parrot tenderly, close to my cheek. Very gently petting its wings. Black wings. I know that just touching lightly, not being possessive, is what opens the way for the little parrot to talk to me in a low-key, conversational way.

Soft words. Words that I see written out, one after the other, on a clean white sheet of paper. Words that the little black parrot and I are saying to each other.

A grey figure flies through grey clouds. It's me. Diving through grey clouds of smoke. I am alone in the grey. The parrot is not with me. I can't see where I've come from. Or where I'm going.

A trapeze swings toward me. I easily take hold of it.

I am with the parrot again. I know that his coming back to me has to do with my overcoming the challenge of flying alone through the grey.

The little black parrot speaks with soft murmuring words. We converse. I am full of awe, wonder at him really talking to me.

I say, "I forgot you could talk."

WHEN I LEFT PRAGUE, I had to give up all that I had loved doing. I was the grey figure in my dream. Alone. Grey thoughts. All my work no longer wanted. Grey. Grey future.

But my dream gives me a trapeze that comes swinging toward me through the thick grey smoke. I easily take hold of it.

I came back to Brownsville and threw all of myself into writing. I was determined to create on paper what I could no longer do with all the wonderful people I'd worked with all over the world.

I am the parrot in my dream. I can still see the bright shining ebony of the wings. My wings.

A parrot with black wings? In the dream the black is not a negative. It's something glorious.

> **parrot,** In the broadest sense, an zygo-
> dactyl of the order Psittaciformes in-
> cluding the parakeets, macaws, lories,
> cockatoos, love birds, and their allies.

> **love bird,** Feeds mostly on soft fruits
> and the honey of flowers.

PART 9

In My Father's Image

34

Hopscotch

OUT MY WINDOW. A sliver of silver shines along the top of the thick black telephone cable. Communication. My life after Papa's death. How to write about it.

OUT MY WINDOW. Dark, etched branches, distinct lines traced against blue/black sky. Like hopscotch lines traced on the black asphalt of the Cherimoya School playground in Hollywood.

> **hopscotch,** [*hop* to leap + *scotch* to scratch a line.] A child's game of hopping on one foot after tossing a disk of stone or fragment of tile from one square to another, traced, or scotched on the ground.

How to write about all the years after Papa's death? I'll toss a fragment and see if I can hop on one foot, pick it up and bring back that one part of my life.

And then another toss.

Bits and pieces that don't make up the whole of my life, but fit into the way this book has traced or scotched itself along so far.

OUT MY WINDOW. The sliver of light on the cable is gone. The sky is lighter. The cable darker.

I can make my toss toward the brightening sky or the black cable. The book lets me choose.

I make a toss.
A long toss.
From 1949, the year of Papa's death.
To 1976.

Renaissance Woman

She's forty-eight years old. She's moved to Oregon.

Her hair is long. Her necklace is turquoise. Her blue jeans faded. Her shirt tie-dyed.

She and her friend Anton, and her three sons, all carpenters, have bought an old false-front store building. They are restoring it to the way it was a hundred years ago.

She drives a VW bus. She's fixed it up with her own carpentry—driftwood bookcases, built-in music speakers, her bed positioned under the Jungian Mandala painted on the ceiling.

Indian feathers—a sacred bird—swinging from the rearview mirror. Dancing to the rhythm of the rattling, rocking bus.

Straight through Oregon.

Heading south.

Down I-5.

Music fills the bus, accompanying her on her journey: the magic of the Beatles, the drone of Bob Dylan, Pink Floyd's haiku lyrics. She sings along with them. Sings and drives and dreams.

Dreams of picking up her mother in Hollywood and bringing her back to Oregon.

Singing and dreaming and driving south, up over the mountains and into California. Planning what she'll say, fashioning the words, the flowing words, words that will inspire her mother to catch the vision of a new life for them. In Oregon. Together.

LOS ANGELES. The bus weaves its way through the tangle of freeways. Before her eyes the daughter sees the new, simple, flower child life. The life that she and her mother will create together.

She loses her way.

As she finally drives into the nursing home parking lot, visiting hours are almost over. She doesn't know her VW bus doesn't fit in with the other cars. The parking attendant tells her to turn off her radio.

The building is large, stucco. This is the last house in Hollywood that her mother will live in.

Inside, the daughter gags at the clinging acid urine smell, hurries by the open doors, sees bony, beckoning hands, hears plaintive cries calling out to her, a bedridden plea: "Come visit a bit?"

She stops in the open door of her mother's room.

Her mother is laid out on the high bed, fenced in with railings, eyes closed, lids fluttering, jaw dropped, mouth gaping wide, breath wheezing in and out.

The daughter steps back from the doorway, her mother wouldn't want to be seen this way.

The daughter turns away, goes down the hall to the water fountain. Returns speaking loudly, although no one is in the hall. "I'm looking for Mrs. Clifton's room. Helen Clifton. My mother."

When she gets back to the door, her mother is ready for her. But not ready for the Oregon trip.

"Why would I do such a thing? You're crazy."

> **crazy,** [Earlier crazed, a variant of crushed, of NORSE origin SW. krasa - to crackle.] **1.** To be broken, crushed, shattered, submitted to violent pressure.

The mother's offhand tone of voice reminds the daughter of the many times her mother has pronounced her crazy.

crazy, 2. To be minutely cracked. In pottery caused by the unequal contraction of the body and the glaze.

When people are crazy, and in disorder,
it's natural for them to groan.

L'Estrange

"Mama, I'm *not* crazy! Not anymore!"

Sitting by the bed, the middle-aged hippie daughter feels real love for her mother. But her words come out in the new Age of Aquarius tongue. A language her mother wants no part of.

"Mama, I want to take you BACK TO THE LAND! With me! And Mama! Mama, I've come to tell you! That no matter what happened in our lives! I now know it's enough that YOU BIRTHED ME!"

The old woman snorts, "You better believe it! If your father had had his way! You'd have been an abortion! But I'd had all the abortions I could take!"

Once again the mother, with one masterful stroke of her tongue, has filled in yet another part of the portrait of the father that she has been painting for the daughter all her life.

DRIVING BACK TO live alone in Oregon, the daughter wonders why she hadn't asked her mother more questions.

"Ask me no questions,
and i'll tell you no lies."

35

My Father's Image

In My Father's Image
Papa probably had this picture taken with this family because they let him
use their farm for location scenes in his silent movie, *Warrens of Virginia*.

The child leaning against Papa's leg seems very content. Papa is looking
tenderly at the baby. But who knows what Papa is thinking? Papa was a
great actor.

> **actor,** One who impersonates a char-
> acter.

> *He (Pitt) was an actor in the Closet,*
> *an actor at Council, and even in*
> *private society he could not lay aside his*
> *theatrical tones and attitudes.*
> Macaulay: *William Pitt*

> *Actor or victim in this wretchedness.*
> Shelley

What was the truth? If Papa did make Mama have abortions, why wasn't
my sister, Pat, an abortion? At that time, movie people had to be above
reproach. Papa's career would be over if the public found out about Mama
being pregnant.

An abortion would have solved everything. Instead, Papa went on the world trip to keep Pat, his first-born child, a secret.

Why? I'll never know.

> He that can discriminate is the father of
> his father.
>
> The Indian Vedas

I made a myth of my father. I created him out of the raw materials of his life. The raw materials are the facts about him that I've written in this book. They are true things that I know happened to him.

But also in the book is the man of my myth. The man in my imagination that I loved, worshipped, lived for. The great rejected artist whom I would save and make be what he was meant to be, when I conquered the forces of evil and set him free.

Dreams Can Come True

Was Papa the man I dreamed him to be? The photographs in the albums say yes. But I've been studying other photographs of other silent stars.

Charismatic images! Magical, mysterious, marvelous images.

Silent images that the early moviegoers saw projected onto the silver screen, glowing in the dark of the movie theater. Images that kept on living in their imaginations as they came out of the theater, blinking in the bright light of day.

Maybe all I really know of my father is the image I projected onto him.

The image of an artist that originated from inside me.
An image I carry of what I am always to be.
The image that has always been me.
Dorinda.

Dorinda, Prague, 1996

36

Big Grey in Venice

A Dream in the Night

It is our back porch. But not the Grace Avenue house. This house is in Venice, Italy. Our back porch is a ledge with steps that lead down into the water of the canal. In the dream I know the canals are so laden with disease-bearing germs, so polluted with sewage, that people who fall in the water will sicken and die.

Big Grey is sitting with me on the ledge. She is the hunter, her head darting this way and that, seeing things in the thick water that I cannot see.

She centers in on something in the water about ten feet out. I hear her make the little clicking noises in her throat that mean she is wanting to go after it.

I'm thinking: Remember, Big Grey, you can't walk on water.

But she does! I see her paws pattering swiftly on the water, leaving behind slight indentations in her path across the water.

I'm thinking: But don't slow down. Your weight will sink you.

She stops. About five feet from me. And she sinks. I see her just below the surface of the water, her face turned to me, her eyes looking up at me. She is perfectly still, no panic, just waiting for me to come and save her.

I think of the pollution of the water. But then I think of how I would feel if I didn't go in after her.

Her eyes waiting. Another moment and it will be too late. I decide I cannot let her die.

The minute I make this decision, I find I don't have to go into the water to do it. I see my hand reaching down under her little body, lifting her up, dangling, dripping, up out of the water. She comes out peacefully, not clawing nor scratching, but trusting me.

I know she will live.

AS I AM WAKING, I am still in my dream and I'm thinking: I hope this teaches her she can't walk on water.

But I know it won't. And I'm glad.

Acknowledgments

My Dictionaries and My Window

acknowledge v. To recognize as a fact or truth, to declare one's belief in. The making public of one's knowledge of something which has been kept back, or concealed; as, to acknowledge a secret marriage, one's faults, one's ignorance.

First, I want to acknowledge my debt to the unknown writers, illustrators, editors who created my hundred year old dictionaries:

Universal Dictionary of the English Language (1899, Peter Fenelon Collier, Publisher)
English Dictionary on Historical Principles (1888, Clarendon Press)
The Century Dictionary (1911, The Century Co.)

The quality of their work was a constant call to me to do my utmost in this book.

Universal Dictionary

OF THE

ENGLISH LANGUAGE

A NEW AND ORIGINAL WORK PRESENTING FOR CONVENIENT REFERENCE THE

ORTHOGRAPHY, PRONUNCIATION, MEANING, USE, ORIGIN AND DEVELOPMENT OF

EVERY WORD IN THE ENGLISH LANGUAGE

TOGETHER WITH

CONDENSED EXPLANATIONS OF FIFTY THOUSAND IMPORTANT SUBJECTS AND AN EXHAUSTIVE ENCYCLOPÆDIA OF ALL THE ARTS AND SCIENCES

PROFUSELY ILLUSTRATED

EDITED BY

ROBERT HUNTER, A.M., F.G.S., AND PROF. CHARLES MORRIS

(ENGLISH EDITION)   (AMERICAN EDITION)

WITH THE ASSISTANCE OF THE FOLLOWING EMINENT SPECIALISTS:

Prof. Thomas H. Huxley, F.R.S.; Prof. Richard A. Proctor; Prof. A. Estoclet; John A. Williams, A.B., Trinity College, Oxford; Sir John Stainer, Mus. Doc.; John Francis Walker, A.M., F.C.S.; T. Davies, F.G.S.; Prof. Seneca Egbert, M.D., Medico-Chirurgical College, Philadelphia; William Harkness, F.I.C., F.R.M.S.; Marcus Benjamin, Ph.D., Smithsonian Institution, Washington, D. C.,

AND ONE HUNDRED OTHERS

VOLUME ONE

NEW YORK

PETER FENELON COLLIER, PUBLISHER

1899

ENGLISH DICTIONARY

ON HISTORICAL PRINCIPLES;

FOUNDED MAINLY ON THᴱ MATERIALS COLLECTED BY

The Philological Society.

EDITED BY

JAMES A. H. MURRAY,

B.A. LOND., HON. M.A. OXON., LL.D. EDIN., D.C.L. DUNELM., ETC.

SOMETIME PRESIDENT OF THE PHILOLOGICAL SOCIETY,

WITH THE ASSISTANCE OF MANY SCHOLARS AND MEN OF SCIENCE.

VOLUME 1 A–BAYWOOD

OXFORD:

AT THE CLARENDON PRESS.

1888.

THE
CENTURY DICTIONARY

AN ENCYCLOPEDIC LEXICON
OF THE ENGLISH LANGUAGE

❧

PREPARED UNDER THE SUPERINTENDENCE OF
WILLIAM DWIGHT WHITNEY, Ph.D., LL.D
LATE PROFESSOR OF COMPARATIVE PHILOLOGY AND SANSKRIT
IN YALE UNIVERSITY

❧

REVISED AND ENLARGED UNDER THE SUPERINTENDENCE OF
BENJAMIN E. SMITH, A.M., L.H.D.
MANAGING EDITOR OF THE FIRST EDITION, AND EDITOR OF THE CENTURY
CYCLOPEDIA OF NAMES, THE CENTURY ATLAS, AND
THE CENTURY DICTIONARY SUPPLEMENT

THE CENTURY CO.
NEW YORK

Lunge, and Parry in Tierce.

Dorinda . . . and . . . Anton

Tony Gorsline (Anton) has had a unique part in the creation of this book. Together we worked through version after version. Line by line. Photo by photo. Choosing from hundreds of old pictures. Copying, recopying, the photos, changing their shapes, sizes, positions on pages. Sometimes with great bursts of emotion. Sometimes the calm between storms. A couple of years of this.

Tony Gorsline is a true, old-fashioned editor with his heart and his money in this project all the way through.

Săng. (From Carl Engel's " Musical Instruments.")

Cheryl Mclean — Amazing book designer.

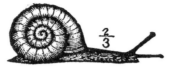

Snail (*Haplotrema concava*).

A PLAY

SCENE ONE: *Dorinda, alone in her one-room, one-window apartment, ponders how to adequately express her appreciation for Cheryl McLean's contribution to the creation of the book.*

SCENE TWO: *Dorinda, talking with her old friend Anton, who is in his backyard laboriously leveling his toolshed.*

DORINDA: Anton, how would you describe what Cheryl has done for my book?

ANTON: What Cheryl has done for your book! Dorinda! She has moved mountains!

CURTAIN
Audience applauds wildly.

Topsail Coasting Schooner.

Chris Anderson—Poet, professor, bheesty.

Bheesty.

Bheesty, n. [Per. Bihishti, lit, heav-enly.] Water carrier, as to a household or a regiment. He carries the water in a mussuk, or skin, usually slung on his back.

Chris was water carrier to me all through the book, even when he had me take out eighty pages. Chris gave me the title: *Woman in the Water.*

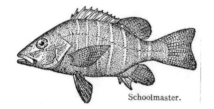

Schoolmaster.

Karen Baldwin—editor, counselor, friend in time of need

Barn Owl (*Tyto alba*).
(½)

Gretchen Sousa—poet, friend of fifty-four years. Gret is my faithful, sensitive, honest, encouraging reader.

Acknowledgment, n. An admission or
a benefit received, courteous recogni-
tion, expression of thanks.

Thoth

My brother, Michael Clifton, and his
wife, Maryann Kuk—for their
laughter and love

My sons Alec, Mark, and Barney Nelson—
for doing a good job of living, so that
I'm free to do my job of writing.

Dagon of the Assyrians. — Bas-re-
lief from Khorsabad.

Chewink.

Bill and Joni Nelson—for all the big
and little ways they help me.

Joseph and Linda DeZurney –
for always being there for me.

Cloudbank Books—for their
contribution to the book.

Photographer Alfred Gescheidt—He wrote that he was delighted to have
this photo in my book. He said it was one of the first he did at the beginning
of his career as a photographer.

"City Cat. Young Tiger Cat. Los Angeles, 1948."
Photo © Alfred Gescheidt

Acknowledgment n. A declaration or avowal of one's act to give it **legal** validity.

I am so grateful to all the copyright holders for granting me permission to use their songs. I am surprised that the words I remember do not always match the words the lyricist wrote; perhaps I was influenced by the rendering a particular singer gave to the song. In this memoir, it seemed important to me to write the words as I remember them.

Songs:

Hard Hearted Hannah (The Vamp of Savannah) by Jack Yellen, Milton Ager, Bob Bigelow and Charles Bates; Copyright 1924 (renewed), Warner Bros. Inc. Rights for extended renewal term in U.S. controlled by Warner Bros., Inc., and Edwin H. Morris & Company, a division of MPI. Communications, Inc. All rights outside the U.S. controlled by Warner Bros., Inc. All rights reserved. Used by permission. Warner Bros. Publications U.S., Inc. (Page 146)

It's Only A Paper Moon by Billy Rose, E. Y. Harburg, Harold Arlen; Copyright 1933 (renewed) Warner Bros., Inc. Rights for extended renewal term in U.S. controlled by Chappell & Co., Glocca Morra Music, and SA Music. All rights outside U.S. controlled by Warner Bros., Inc. All rights reserved. Used by permission. Warner Bros. Publications U.S., Inc. (Page 162)

Love (Can Be a Moment's Madness) by Ralph Blane and Hugh Martin, Copyright 1945 (renewed) EMI Feist Catalog Inc. All rights reserved. Used by permission. Warner Bros. Publications U.S., Inc. (Page 172)

Some Enchanted Evening, Copyright © 1949 by Richard Rogers and Oscar Hammerstein II. Copyright renewed, Williamson Music, owner of publication and allied rights throughout the world. International copyright secured. All rights reserved. Used by permission. (Page 172)

They Say It's Wonderful by Irving Berlin. Copyright © 1946 by Irving Berlin. Copyright Renewed. International copyright secured. All rights reserved. Reprinted by permission. (Page 173)

Bucking Bronco.

Snapping Turtle (*Chelydra serpentina*).

Newspaper Articles/Photos:

Photos:

Grasshopper of the family Locustidae. *Locusta viridissima* of Europe.

About the Author

Frances Timpone Weppler

BORN IN HOLLYWOOD, Dorinda Clifton trained as a dancer, worked in Fred Astaire and Gene Kelly musicals, and was leading lady in Columbia's *Girl of the Limberlost* and Hopalong Cassidy's *Marauders*.

In Prague in 1990–97, Dorinda worked with Jaroslav Ducek, director of the drama department of the Jesek Conservatory of Music. She spent her summers in New Zealand, working with a band of young musicians, creating rock operas that toured Asia and Europe. In 1985–89, Dorinda went in and out of Eastern Europe, working with young performing artists who were living under communist dictatorships.

Dorinda is now working on a novel, *The Michelangelo Mandate—A Present-day Gothic Tale*, and an as-yet-untitled sequel to *Woman in the Water*.